Free Soil Party (Mass.)

Reunion of the Free Soilers of 1848-1852 at the Parker House, Boston, Massachusetts

June 28, 1888

Free Soil Party (Mass.)

Reunion of the Free Soilers of 1848-1852 at the Parker House, Boston, Massachusetts
June 28, 1888

ISBN/EAN: 9783744753432

Printed in Europe, USA, Canada, Australia, Japan

Cover: Foto ©ninafisch / pixelio.de

More available books at **www.hansebooks.com**

REUNION

OF THE

FREE SOILERS OF 1848-1852

AT THE PARKER HOUSE,

BOSTON, MASSACHUSETTS,

June 28, 1888.

———

CAMBRIDGE:

JOHN WILSON AND SON.

University Press.

1888.

.

CONTENTS.

	PAGE
CIRCULAR OF INVITATION	. 9
LIST OF PERSONS PRESENT .	10
DINNER . . .	13
ADDRESS OF Hon. EDWARD L. PIERCE	. 14
" " Hon. SAMUEL E. SEWALL .	22
" Col. THOMAS W. HIGGINSON	24
" " Hon. FRANCIS W. BIRD .	28
" " Hon. STEPHEN H. PHILLIPS	30
" " Gen. JOHN L. SWIFT .	34
" " EDWARD ATKINSON, Esq.	38
" Hon. JOHN WINSLOW .	43
" Col. W. S. B. HOPKINS .	51
" " Hon. HORACE E. SMITH .	53
" " JOHN C. WYMAN, Esq.	56
" " THOMAS DREW, Esq.	60
" " HENRY H. CHAMBERLAIN, Esq.	62
APPOINTMENT OF COMMITTEE OF PUBLICATION .	64

APPENDIX.

REMARKS OF CALEB A. WALL .	65
" " Hon. MILTON M. FISHER	70
LETTER FROM Dr. HENRY I. BOWDITCH	72
" " JOHN G. WHITTIER	72
" " Hon. GEORGE F. HOAR .	73
" " Judge E. R. HOAR	73
PARTIAL LIST OF THE FREE SOILERS OF 1848-1852 .	74
REUNION OF THE FREE SOILERS OF FRANKLIN COUNTY	84

REUNION

OF THE

FREE SOILERS OF 1848-1852.

Who reverenced his conscience as his king,
Whose glory was redressing human wrong.
TENNYSON.

Ah, well! — The world is discreet;
    There are plenty to pause and wait:
But here was a man who set his feet
    Sometimes in advance of fate, —

Plucked off the old bark when the inner
    Was slow to renew it,
And put to the Lord's work the sinner
    When saints failed to do it.

Never rode to the wrong's redressing
    A worthier paladin:
Shall he not hear the blessing,
    " Good and faithful, enter in ! "
WHITTIER.

Every age on him who strays
From its broad and beaten ways,
    Pours its sevenfold vial.

Happy he whose inward ear
Angel comfortings can hear
    O'er the rabble's laughter;
And while Hatred's fagots burn,
Glimpses through the smoke discern
    Of the good hereafter.

Knowing this, that never yet
Share of Truth was vainly set
    In the world's wide fallow;
After hands shall sow the seed,
After hands from hill and mead
    Reap the harvests yellow.
WHITTIER.

FREE SOIL REUNION AT BOSTON.

THE FORTIETH ANNIVERSARY of the first State Convention of the FREE SOILERS OF MASSACHUSETTS occurring on the 28th of June of the present year, it was decided by some of the surviving members of that organization to call together as many of the representative men of that famous party still living as could be conveniently provided for at a Boston hotel; and with this view the following circular was sent to about three hundred of the Free Soilers in the State, whose addresses could be obtained:

FREE SOILERS OF MASSACHUSETTS.
1848–1852.

THE Fortieth Anniversary of the meeting of the Convention at Worcester which formed the Free Soil Party of Massachusetts, will be commemorated by the survivors of the party by a dinner at Young's Hotel, in Boston, on

THURSDAY, JUNE 28, NEXT,

at 1 P.M. A room will be open at 11 A.M. of that day, to give guests an opportunity for friendly meeting and conversation.

You, as one of the survivors of that noble and historical party, are invited to participate in the occasion. The price of tickets will be Three Dollars ; and as the number is limited, preference will be given to those who first accept. Please communicate, on or before June 20, your reply to Henry O. Hildreth, Room 12, 82 Devonshire Street, Boston, who will supply the tickets.

WILLIAM CLAFLIN.	FRANCIS W. BIRD.
T. W. HIGGINSON.	ADIN THAYER.
EBEN F. STONE.	EDWARD L. PIERCE.

BOSTON, June 5, 1888.

2

In response to this invitation, the following named gentlemen (one hundred and fourteen in number) assembled at the Parker House[1] on Thursday, June 28, 1888: —

ROBERT ADAMS	Fall River.
DANIEL W. ALLEN	Lynn.
STEPHEN M. ALLEN	Duxbury.
EDWARD ATKINSON	Boston.
JOHN BACKUP	Roxbury.
ISAAC H. BAILEY	New York City.
GEORGE M. BAKER	Marshfield.
JOHN N. BARBOUR	Cambridge.
SAMUEL D. BARDWELL	Shelburne Falls.
CHARLES T. BARRY	Boston.
DAVID B. BARTLETT	Lowell.
WINSLOW BATTLES	Randolph.
FRANCIS W. BIRD	Walpole.
MATTHEW BOLLES	West Roxbury.
JOHN BOTUME	Boston.
THOMAS T. BOUVÉ	Boston.
ALBERT G. BROWNE	Boston.
SAMUEL M. BUBIER	Lynn.
THOMAS F. BURGESS	Lowell.
JONATHAN BUTTERFIELD	Dorchester.
JAMES S. CAMPBELL	Newton.
JOSIAH H. CARTER	Dorchester.
GEORGE N. CATE	Marlborough.
HENRY H. CHAMBERLAIN	Worcester.
ASAPH CHURCHILL	Dorchester.
CHARLES M. S. CHURCHILL	Milton.
ARTHUR B. CLAFLIN	Newton.
LUCIUS CLAPP	Stoughton.
ASA CLEMENT	Dracut.
JAMES B. COLLINGWOOD	Plymouth.

[1] The place of meeting was changed from Young's Hotel to the Parker House in order to secure a larger dining-hall.

Joshua E. Crane . . . . Bridgewater.
Isaac H. Cushing . . . . Hingham.
Charles G. Davis . . . . Plymouth.
Robert T. Davis . . . . Fall River.
Thomas Drew . . . . Newton.
George E. Eaton . . . . Needham.
Charles Endicott . . . . Canton.
William Endicott, Jr. . . . . . . Boston.
Alonzo H. Evans . . . . Everett.
John S. Farlow . . . . Newton.
Milton M. Fisher . . . . Medway.
Hiram M. French . . . . Boston.
Thomas Gaffield . . . . Boston.
Cyrus Gale . . . . Northborough.
John Girdler . . . . Beverly.
Daniel W. Gooch . . . . Melrose.
Henry Guild . . . . Boston.
Christopher A. Hack . . . . Taunton.
James G. Hartshorn . . . . Walpole.
Joseph K. Hayes . . . . Cambridge.
John C. Haynes . . . . Boston.
Charles A. Hewins . . . . West Roxbury.
Thomas W. Higginson . . . . . . Cambridge.
Henry O. Hildreth . . . . Dedham.
Milo Hildreth . . . . Northborough.
Eli W. Holbrook . . . . West Boylston.
Aaron Hook . . . . Charlestown.
William S. B. Hopkins . . . . . . Worcester.
Joseph A. Howland . . . . Worcester.
Clarke Jillson . . . . Worcester.
Peter Johnson . . . . Lynn.
William H. S. Jordan . . . . . . Boston.
Martin P. Kennard . . . . . . Brookline.
Franklin King . . . . Dorchester.
Edward W. Kinsley . . . . Boston.
Chauncy L. Knapp . . . . Lowell.
John Kneeland . . . . Roxbury.
Seth Mann . . . . . . Randolph.

ORAMEL MARTIN	Worcester.
JOHN J. MAY	Dorchester.
ANDREW McPHAIL	Boston.
BENJAMIN MERRIAM	West Roxbury.
JOHN J. MERRILL	Roxbury.
AUSTIN MESSENGER	Norton.
ELISHA C. MONK	Stoughton.
MARCUS MORTON	Andover.
CURTIS C. NICHOLS	Cambridge.
JOHN A. NOWELL	Boston.
EDWIN PATCH	Lynn.
STEPHEN H. PHILLIPS	Salem.
WILLIAM PHILLIPS	Lynn.
EDWARD L. PIERCE	Milton.
GEORGE W. POPE	Boston.
HIRAM A. PRATT	Somerville.
LABAN PRATT	Dorchester.
NATHAN B. PRESCOTT	Roxbury.
DAVID PULSIFER	Boston.
JOSIAH M. READ	Boston.
OLIVER W. ROBBINS	Pittsfield.
GEORGE W. RUSSELL	Worcester.
WILLARD SEARS	Newton.
SAMUEL E. SEWALL	Melrose.
CHARLES A. B. SHEPARD	Boston.
ELIJAH SHUTE	Hingham.
HORACE E. SMITH	Albany, N. Y.
CHARLES A. STEVENS	Ware.
EBEN F. STONE	Newburyport.
JOHN L. SWIFT	Roxbury.
DAVID THAYER	Boston.
ALBERT TOLMAN	Worcester.
WILLIAM B. TRASK	Dorchester.
SAMSON R. URBINO	Roxbury.
EDWIN WALDEN	Lynn.
CALEB A. WALL	Worcester.
WILLIAM A. WALLACE	Canaan, N. H.
JOHN W. WETHERELL	Worcester.

ALFRED WILLIAMS . . . . Roxbury.
JOHN WINSLOW . . . . Brooklyn, N. Y.
BARTHOLOMEW WOOD . . . . Newton.
ROLAND WORTHINGTON . . . . Roxbury.
STEPHEN C. WRIGHTINGTON . . . . . . Fall River.
JOHN C. WYMAN. . . . . Valley Falls, R. I.
JAMES M. W. YERRINGTON . . . . Boston.
WILLIAM F. YOUNG . . . . Wakefield.

Two hours, from 11 A.M. to 1 P.M., were devoted to the interchange of congratulations and the renewal of old friendships. The presence of John G. Whittier, who notwithstanding his advanced age and infirm health could not lose this opportunity of meeting his old friends and associates, added greatly to the pleasure of the occasion. The interdict of his physician alone prevented Mr. Whittier's attendance at the dinner.

Promptly at 1 o'clock P.M. Hon. EDWARD L. PIERCE, of Milton, President of the day, led the way to the large dining-hall, where plates had been laid for one hundred and ten guests. Mr. PIERCE took the head of the table, and near him were seated Chief-Justice Morton, Hon. Horace E. Smith, Hon. Samuel E. Sewall, Hon. Francis W. Bird, Col. Thomas W. Higginson, Hon. Robert T. Davis, Hon. Eben F. Stone, Hon. John Winslow, and others. The dinner, which was served in the best style of the famous Parker House, lasted for an hour and a half, when the company was called to order by Mr. PIERCE, who then proceeded to make the opening address of the occasion as follows : —

ADDRESS OF HON. EDWARD L. PIERCE.

VETERAN FREE SOILERS OF MASSACHUSETTS! Forty years ago you rallied for the defence of freedom in the United States. Forty years ago this day, in the city of Worcester, under the open sky, to the number of thousands, the free-men of the Commonwealth, coming from all its counties, met with one inspiration, and declared by formal resolutions and the voices of eloquent orators their determination to resist the extension of slavery to another foot of American soil. Breaking all political bonds, they took their stand against existing parties, against the slave interest of the South and the organized capital of the North, and set up a new and independent power in American politics. They listened on that day, with Samuel Hoar in the chair, to resolutions reported by Stephen C. Phillips, and to addresses from Charles Francis Adams, Charles Sumner, Henry Wilson, Amasa Walker, Joshua Leavitt, Edward L. Keyes, E. Rockwood Hoar, Lewis D. Campbell, and Joshua R. Giddings, — all save one now numbered with the dead. That assembly combined what is always best in our old and beloved Commonwealth, — that conscience, that intelligence, and that faith in humanity which are her hereditary glory. The survivors of the Free Soil party of Massachusetts meet at this hour to mourn no lost cause, but to commemorate a movement at once glorious and triumphant. We come not here to lament the dead, or to indulge in regrets that our own lives are passing. Rather with full hearts let us rejoice that God gave us the privilege of serving such a cause, under such leaders, and with such associates.

The proceedings which resulted in the convention of June, 1848, deserve a brief reference. The Antislavery Whigs, known as " Conscience Whigs," who made resistance to slavery the paramount issue, had been from 1845

to 1848 in conflict with the "Cotton Whigs," who treated
that issue as subordinate to the maintenance of the tariff
and the financial measures of the Whig party. Some of
you recall the Whig State conventions of 1846 and 1847, in
both of which Mr. Webster appeared, with Palfrey, Adams,
Sumner, and Phillips on the one side, and Winthrop on the
other. In May, 1848, Mr. Adams called a conference at
his office, which was attended by Phillips, Sumner, Wilson,
Keyes, E. R. Hoar, Francis W. Bird, and Edward Wall-
cutt, where a call drawn by Mr. Hoar for a convention was
agreed upon, to be issued in case the Whig convention at
Philadelphia should refuse to adopt the principle of exclud-
ing slavery from the territories, and should nominate a
candidate not openly committed to such exclusion. The
Philadelphia convention rejected a resolution affirming
that principle, and nominated General Taylor for President. Promptly Charles Allen announced, "The Whig
party is here and this day dissolved!" and, referring to
the conciliatory offer of the vice-presidency to Massachusetts, added with emphasis and scorn, "Massachusetts will
spurn the bribe!" Wilson followed with the historic protest, "So help me God, I will do all I can to defeat the
election of that candidate!" He called at once a conference of those who were ready to act with him, and fifteen
attended, of whom only two survive, — Stanley Matthews
of Ohio, now a justice of the Supreme Court of the United
States, and John C. Vaughan of the same State, a retired
editor, now living in Cincinnati. Allen and Wilson were
true to their word, and immediately on their return home
appealed to their constituents by address and letter. The
call for the convention at Worcester, already drawn and
held in reserve, was issued, and forthwith one of the most
remarkable agitations in our history ensued. Old men and
young men, and women also, joined in the new movement
with all the ardor of crusaders, and the air rang with the

voices of freedom from the Berkshire hills to the sea. Of the officers of the Worcester convention, all are gone. Of the speakers, none but Judge Hoar survives. Of the committee on platform, of which Mr. Phillips was chairman, only Judge Hoar and Milton M. Fisher, of Medway, are living. The latter, whose Antislavery work goes back to 1833, fifty-five years ago, is with us to-day. Of the delegates chosen for the State or districts to attend the national Free Soil convention at Buffalo, only Josiah G. Abbott, John A. Kasson, Chauncey L. Knapp, and Mr. Fisher survive. Mr. Adams presided over the mass convention at Buffalo; and his presence at one of its sessions being required elsewhere, he withdrew from the chair, calling to it Francis W. Bird, a veteran whom we greet to-day.

The greatness of the issue which brought the Free Soil party into existence appears when we recall the fact that at that time the population of the country, slightly exceeding twenty millions, was, with the exception of Texas, limited to the States east of the Mississippi and to the four States contiguous to its western shore. Beyond the great river Iowa alone was secure to freedom; all else was territory with destiny undetermined. The propagandists of slavery demanded, with threats of disunion and armed resistance, that the territories — those recently acquired from Mexico and those included in the Louisiana purchase — should be opened to slavery. That vast region, then uninhabited, but now swarming with population, imperial in space, stretching from the western boundaries of Iowa and Missouri to the Pacific Ocean, and from the British possessions to the Mexican line, with untold mineral and agricultural wealth, was in peril. Contemplate its territorial magnitude and its capacity as a seat of empire! It embraced more than sixteen hundred thousand square miles, — five times as many as were included in the original thirteen States, and more than half of our entire dominion before the

later purchase of Alaska. It was altogether unrecognized in
the census of 1840, and was reported in that of 1850 with
only two hundred thousand inhabitants, chiefly natives and
new settlers in California and New Mexico. To-day it
numbers not less than seven millions of people, more than
a third of the entire population of the United States in
1848, — a number which, in view of the western movement of the mass of emigrants from continental Europe, is
likely to rise to twenty-five millions within the lifetime of
men now living. Truly the Free Soilers of 1848 did not
exaggerate when they warned the people that the destinies
of countless millions were at stake. Their movement saved
Oregon, which under its pressure was organized as a free
territory immediately on the adjournment of the Buffalo
convention. It concentrated the Antislavery sentiment of
the North against the extension of slavery. It stood defiant
when the two old parties declared the compromise measures
of 1850 a finality, and attempted to crush out all agitation
against them. It prepared the way for that larger movement which came near success in 1856, and finally triumphed in 1860. History commemorates it as one of the
stages in that grand conflict with slavery which made our
country free from ocean to ocean, with no master and no
slave in any part of its domain. Sumner expressed its
significance at the time: " We found now a new party.
Its corner-stone is freedom. Its broad, all-sustaining arches
are truth, justice, and humanity."

The specific object of the Free Soil movement of 1848
was the exclusion of slavery from the territories ; but its
idea and spirit were broader. Its platform at Buffalo,
largely the work of Salmon P. Chase, assisted by Charles
Francis Adams and Benjamin F. Butler, of New York,
called for legislation by Congress against slavery wherever
it depended on national law. Satisfied with this compre-
hensive declaration, the Liberty party, which had cast seven

thousand votes in 1840 and sixty-two thousand in 1844, in each case for James G. Birney, joined in the new party, which, with Van Buren and Adams as candidates, cast two hundred and ninety-one thousand in 1848. Their numbers were reduced in 1852 to one hundred and fifty-six thousand, chiefly by the return of the Barnburners of New York to the Democratic party. In Massachusetts the party maintained its vigor until the election of 1854, when it was distracted by the Know-Nothing controversy. A year or two later it was merged in the Republican party, which grew out of the repeal of the Missouri Compromise.

The Free Soilers of Massachusetts were men of extraordinary vitality. Not only their foremost leaders, but their chief men in towns and cities were strong in their combination of intellect, will, and intense moral convictions. Casting less than forty thousand votes at their highest point, and falling at times below thirty thousand, less than a third of the voters of the State, it is noteworthy how many of them afterward came to the front rank in public life. Samuel Hoar, Horace Mann, Stephen C. Phillips, and Edward L. Keyes died before the war; but the other leaders lived to take part in the civil conflicts which ended in the entire abolition of slavery in the United States. The Legislature chosen in 1850 placed Sumner in the Senate, where he remained till his death, in 1874, always the Antislavery protagonist in Congress, and for ten years chairman of the Committee on Foreign Relations. Wilson became his colleague in 1855, succeeding Edward Everett, served as chairman of the committee on Military Affairs during the war, and when he died, in 1875, was holding the second office under the Constitution of the United States. Adams, entering Congress by an election in 1858, was soon called to represent the country as its ambassador to Great Britain, and to conduct the most important diplomatic controversy in our history; the public

spirit inherited from his ancestors he transmitted to his
sons, two of whom were old enough to give their youthful
sympathies to the Free Soil cause. Charles Allen was
chosen to a seat in Congress, and later served for a long
period as chief-justice of the Superior Court. E. Rockwood
Hoar has served as justice of the Supreme Court of the
State, member of Congress, and attorney-general of the
United States. Anson Burlingame, after service in Congress, became our minister to China, and was adopted by
that country as its ambassador to European nations and
our own. Richard H. Dana, Jr., as United States district
attorney and author, assisted in the just settlement of most
important questions of international law, and was nominated
minister to England, his confirmation being defeated only
by personal malignity. John A. Andrew became illustrious as governor of the State during the Civil War, and
after an interval William Claflin was his successor in that
office. Marcus Morton, of Taunton, an old Jeffersonian
Democrat, came with his three gifted sons into the movement; and the one bearing his name and inheriting his
judicial faculty has had a career of thirty years on the
bench, and now holds the high office of chief-justice of the
Commonwealth: we gratefully recognize his presence at this
table to-day. To the roll of members of Congress has
been added from the party, besides names already mentioned, those of George F. Hoar, of Worcester, now our
senator in Congress, and one of the foremost in that great
body; John A. Kasson, of New Bedford, at one time minister to Austria; Alexander De Witt, of Oxford; Amasa
Walker, of North Brookfield; John D. Baldwin and William
W. Rice, both of Worcester; Chauncey L. Knapp, of Lowell;
Daniel W. Gooch, of Melrose; John B. Alley, of Lynn;
Eben F. Stone, of Newburyport; Henry L. Pierce, of Dorchester; and Robert T. Davis, of Fall River. One of the
most gifted of the Free Soilers of 1848 was Erastus Hop-

kins, of the Connecticut valley, ever to be remembered as
an orator of rare grace and power, and a steady and unselfish advocate of freedom; we are glad to recognize his
features and genius in his son, a leader of the bar of Massachusetts, and present with us.

But I must not prolong the enumeration. Time would
fail me to tell of Gideon and of Barak, and of Sam-
son and of Jephthah, of David also, and Samuel, and
of the Prophets, who through faith stood firm for the freedom of a race, wrought righteousness, out of weakness
were made strong, waxed valiant in fight, breasted social
and political proscription, and served faithfully a cause as
holy as any for which martyrs have died. We have with
us as participants in this reunion two distinguished men,
whose Antislavery service exceeds a half century in duration, — John G. Whittier, the poet of freedom, now of
four-score years; and Samuel E. Sewall, still older, the
Nestor of the Massachusetts bar, born in the last year of
the last century. We welcome with tender regard the
author of those inspiring hymns which touched the hearts
of millions of freemen and broke the fetters of the slave;
we honor the patriarch of the law, whose services were
always at the command of fugitive slaves before hostile or
unsympathetic tribunals. In this connection I ought to
recall to you that the Liberty party cast one thousand votes
for its first candidate for governor in 1841, and nearly
thirty-five hundred the next year; and that from 1843
to 1847 inclusive — five successive years — the standard-
bearer was Samuel E. Sewall, whose vote rose from six
thousand to nearly ten thousand; his modesty and self-
abnegation have alone kept him from being called to high
public trusts. We are fortunate, too, in the presence of
Horace E. Smith, formerly of Chelsea, now dean of the
Law School at Albany; of John Winslow, formerly of
Newton, now an eminent citizen and lawyer of Brooklyn,

N. Y.; and of Francis W. Bird, who at the age of seventy-eight retains the freshness and vitality of youth. One word for the absent, whom necessity and not their choice prevents their mingling in this festivity, — Annis Merrill, of Boston, who emigrated to California in 1849, and now lives in San Francisco; Shubael P. Adams, of Lowell, who has lived since 1857 in Dubuque, Iowa; John A. Kasson, of New Bedford, long a resident of the same State; and Herman Kreissman, of Boston, later of Chicago, once consul-general to Germany, and now residing in Berlin. Among others necessarily absent are John B. Alley, now travelling abroad; William Claflin, who engaged his seat with us, but was at the last moment kept away by a disability resulting from a recent accident; Henry L. Pierce, who is on his way to Europe; Judge Hoar, who is seeking health at Sharon Springs; and his brother, the senator, engaged in public business at Washington.

A reunion of the Free Soilers of Massachusetts took place at Melville Garden, in Hingham, August 9, 1877, — the twenty-ninth anniversary of the convention at Buffalo, where many here to-day, and others no longer living, were the guests of the late Samuel Downer. This second reunion, it is altogether probable, will be the last celebration of that historic movement. Allow me to add one suggestion. This occasion is commemorative, and has no relation to present controversies or divisions. The heats of youth are passed, and we can all well afford, however we may now be parted in our political relations, to give this day to common memories of a great struggle in which we stood shoulder to shoulder in defence of human liberty on this continent.

Mr. PIERCE's speech was frequently interrupted by applause, — mention of the names of Phillips, Sumner, Wilson, Sewall, Bird, and of the poet

Whittier, who had left the reception room a few moments before the dinner, being particularly well received.

THE PRESIDENT: By right of his advanced age and priority of service, SAMUEL E. SEWALL should have the first place in the order of speeches, and I now call upon him to address you.

REMARKS OF HON. SAMUEL E. SEWALL.

MR. CHAIRMAN AND BROTHER FREE SOILERS, — I ought not to allow myself to be called upon, as I have made no preparation for a speech. Still, I could not refuse the request when I was asked by the president a short time ago, and so I speak, though I have very little to say.

Gentlemen, we were engaged not only in a righteous fight, but in a most delightful one. We enjoyed, I doubt not, the contest in those days. We must rejoice now that we were engaged in that contest, and that we still survive to enjoy its memories at the present time. But, as I said in the beginning, I have only to express the satisfaction which I feel at being here and among you. I will, however, say one word in advocacy of a cause which is exactly analogous to this matter of the emancipation of slavery, and that is this: I recommend to the attention of all who are here present the emancipation of women. Old Cato, whenever he ended a speech in the Roman Senate, was sure to add: "This I say, and Carthage must be destroyed!" So I finish by saying, The emancipation of women must be carried!

A hearty round of applause was given Mr. Sewall as he sat down.

THE PRESIDENT: It was observed that as we took our seats some gentlemen waited, as if in a reverent mood, for some one to say grace; and it is fitting to explain why no one rose to perform the service. The Rev. Dr. James Freeman Clarke, who served as chaplain at Downer's Landing in 1877, had been designated for the same office on this occasion; but we were called to mourn his death on the eighth day of this month. We then applied to the Rev. Dr. Andrew P. Peabody, of Cambridge, who in 1848 was the pastor of a church in Portsmouth, N. H. Early in the month of August of that year he wrote an open letter to a friend, in which, replying to the assertion that it was always a duty to choose between two evils rather than make one's action ineffective, he said that he recognized no such duty under the circumstances, and that if the alternative in the pending election were to be between Moloch and Belial, he should take his place with Gabriel and the "scattering" voters. To our regret, Dr. Peabody, though sympathetic with our commemoration to-day, and anxious to be with us, was obliged to decline in favor of a previous engagement at the anniversary exercises of Harvard College. We were then unable to recall any other survivor of 1848 who could appropriately fill the vacant place of the lamented Dr. Clarke.

In 1848 two young men led the Free Soilers of Newburyport and Essex north, — Colonel EBEN F. STONE, and Colonel, then Reverend, THOMAS W. HIGGINSON, both with us to-day. I now present to you the latter.

ADDRESS OF THOMAS W. HIGGINSON.

MR. CHAIRMAN, — A small boy in the story asked his father, who looked a little depressed at breakfast, what was the matter with him. He replied that he was depressed because he had that day to engineer a public meeting. "Why," said the boy, "I should think that would be easy enough. All you have got to do is to turn on the cranks." Now you, Mr. Chairman, have not merely to turn on the cranks, but to get together a body composed of men every one of whom was considered a crank forty years ago. And he probably was one in his secret soul, and is as much of a crank to-day as he was half a century ago. That is the sort of quality that does not get out of a man. Talk about the heats of youth! They go out of us; but we have all to struggle with the heats of age, which are much harder to conquer than the heats of youth. Look at our dear old friend Sewall, who has just launched us all into another cause, whether we espouse it or no. It is the way these reformers are made; there is no getting it out of them. Lord Bacon said, in his essay on "Youth and Age," — he is a man of whom you may probably have heard: a man whose plays, it is claimed, are performed at our theatres, — Lord Bacon said that heat and vivacity in age make the best of all compositions for business. And if you doubt it, apply to Mr. Sewall or Mr. Francis Bird.

We have come here, Mr. Chairman, looking back on forty years ago, to write in a manner the epitaph of a movement with which we were then identified; and that is practically the same thing as writing our own epitaph. We have it on the authority of one of the men who came near being nominated for President at Chicago, but was not, that every man ought to write his own epitaph, because no one is usu-

ally so familiar with the virtues of the deceased. Mr. Depew
was right; and it is the same with us to-day. If we do not
spend the afternoon in speaking well of ourselves, we shall
waste it. Do not imagine that we can rely on any one else
to do it for us. However great any movement may be, it
will rarely bring immortality to those who take part in it.
The rewards of great actions do not come in that form.
What great agitation in England is known by the names
of more than one or two leaders? That great movement
which led to the emancipation of the slaves in the West
Indies, an agitation which broke up families and beggared
wealthy men, — how much is left of the individuals taking
part in it, except the bare names of Wilberforce and Clark-
son? All the rest are forgotten. The great history of the
English Corn-law agitation shows the same thing; we know
only the names of Cobden and Bright, Bright and Cobden.
If we are to find our reward in the shape of personal
fame, we shall probably never have it; that comes only to
the few. Of all the men concerned in that great Free
Soil movement, perhaps the only one man who will go
down to immortality is Charles Sumner. And the names
of those who will be linked with his, will be one or two of
the men who denounced us; but they were men like Garrison and Phillips, of whom we were glad to learn, even
while they reproved us. How many of the heroes our
chairman commemorated are now even remembered by the
press? How great were the services of John G. Palfrey!
I remember speaking to him on his own doorstep, when
he said to me: "The hard thing is not to encounter the
denunciations of the newspapers or of public opinion; the
hard thing to bear is the attitude of men who have loved
you, and whom you have loved all your life, and who pass
you by in the streets without speaking to you." What is
his reward in history? Why, Stedman, in his book on the
poets of the United States, mistakenly enumerates him

4

among the " doughfaces " whom Lowell satirizes ; and Dr.
Peabody of Cambridge says of him in his " Reminiscences "
that he was defeated for Congress because his Antislavery
views were not sufficiently pronounced ! How firmly Theodore Parker planted his feet on the earth ! He left a
record which it seemed would be illustrious even for one
hundred years, its praises sounded and its brightness never
to be dimmed. Yet on looking at the last edition of
the one great dictionary of biography of the world, the
French " Biographie Générale," you will find that Theodore
Parker was an eminent Boston clergyman, who devoted his
life to vindicating the infallibility of the Holy Scriptures
and the deity of our Lord Jesus !

These things illustrate how little the most heroic action
avails to secure the reward of permanent fame. Its reward comes, if anywhere, in the satisfaction of seeing a
great result secured.

Forty years ago we undertook a certain work, which no
disguises of history can put out of sight ; and that work is
done. I went a week or two ago, for the first time in
thirty-two years, across the plains to Kansas. I revisited
the scenes of the struggle, which some of you contributed
money to support, in order to vindicate the right of freedom
at that time. I saw across those prairies stately cities that
have risen, with universities, public halls and libraries,
where, thirty-two years ago, I left only the few log-huts
occupied by the few emigrants supported by the charity —
no, the patriotism — of Massachusetts. I left those prairies then without a tree. I came back, and found them
without a slave. That was the record of these thirty-two
years, all proceeding remotely, — not so very remotely, —
proceeding legitimately from the modest movement which
was initiated in that State so long ago. In the presence of
results so important as the final abolition of slavery, what
is any man's reputation ? Who cares for fame ? Who

cares for individuals, except that they furnish friendships
which support us even in sorrow and discouragement?
Who cares for anything in the past except the magnificence
of its results? It was the joy of the men who engaged in
it while it lasted ; and we come together to-day to look on
one another's faces, perhaps for the last time, but feeling
that the work in which we took part was rich and strong,
and worthy of American humanity.

I have only one thing more to say, Mr. Chairman. This
I wish to say, with the understanding that whatever dis-
aster may befall, no blame is to attach to you as the con-
ductor. I remember what Sam Weller said timidly to his
father when he wrote his love-letter to Mary : " I might
end it with a werse." His father objected, but Sam per-
sisted, and ended it : " Your love-sick Pickwick." I am
going to end this speech with a verse, or only three verses
at the longest.

The speaker then proceeded to read the following
original poem, entitled —

WAITING FOR THE BUGLE.

We wait for the bugle ; the night-dews are cold,
The limbs of the soldiers feel jaded and old ;
The field of our bivouac is windy and bare,
There is lead in our joints, there is frost in our hair ;
The future is veiled and its fortunes unknown
As we lie with hushed breath till the bugle is blown.

At the sound of that bugle each comrade shall spring
Like an arrow released from the strain of the string ;
The courage, the impulse of youth shall come back
To banish the chill of the drear bivouac ;
And sorrows and losses and cares fade away
When that life-giving signal proclaims the new day.

Though the bivouac of age may put ice in our veins,
And no fibre of steel in our sinew remains ;
Though the comrades of yesterday's march are not here,
And the sunlight seems pale and the branches are sere ;
Though the sound of our cheering dies down to a moan, —
We shall find our lost youth when the bugle is blown.

The speech of Colonel Higginson and the beautiful poem with which it concluded, were deeply appreciated and warmly applauded by the audience.

THE PRESIDENT : We shall now listen to FRANCIS W. BIRD, of Walpole, whose early service, already referred to, is familiar to you all.

ADDRESS OF HON. FRANCIS W. BIRD.

MEN AND BRETHREN ! FELLOW INDEPENDENTS OF 1848 ! How freshly this gathering reminds us of what it cost to be Independents in those days ! But history repeats itself.

When you told me, Mr. Chairman, that you would expect me to say a few words to our old comrades to-day, in rummaging my memory for the text, I fell upon this from the " Lady of the Lake," —

" How are they blotted from the things that be !
   How few, all weak and withered of their force,
 Wait on the verge of dark eternity,
   Like stranded wrecks, the tide returning hoarse
 To sweep them from our sight !   Time rolls his ceaseless course."

But your subsequent hint, " Give us a speech in a cheerful strain," prohibited notes more natural to an octogenarian. *Hæc olim meminisse juvabit*, — be this rather the key-note.

Reference has been made to my having presided over the Buffalo convention in 1848. This happened from the accident of my standing near Mr. Adams when he was called out to attend a meeting of a committee. As he left the chair, he whispered to me, " Fred Douglass wants to speak, but these Barnburners don't want a colored man to appear on the platform." Others advised me not to recognize him. My reply was, " If Mr. Douglass addresses the chair, he shall have the floor ; " and he did.

As an illustration of the proscription which befell the Independents of those times, let me mention one incident. Walking down Beacon Street with Dr. Palfrey, he said, " The time was when, if I found myself about dinner-time without any particular place to dine, I had only to ring one of these door-bells, and I was sure of a welcome ; but now it is a long time since my legs have been under any of their mahogany."

In recalling the history of those twenty years from 1848 (eliminating three or four years of the demoralizing up-heaval of Know Nothingism, — " Young America on a spree "), I love to dwell upon the unselfish, self-forgetful characters of the leading Free Soilers and early Republi-cans, — yes, even of the politicians. " The machine " had not then been invented, at least for us. With the excep-tion of Henry Wilson's election to the United States senate by the Know Nothing legislature of 1855, no important public office in Massachusetts was ever disposed of as " truck and dicker."

My friends, who of us does not feel what a benediction it has been to us to have lived in those times and with those men ? Who does not feel that if we have done the State any service, it has been largely due to the education we received from them ? To all of them may be applied, with almost equal truth, what I said some years ago of two of them, — Samuel G. Howe, and John A. Andrew (pardon me for quoting myself) : " These great and good men seemed utterly unconscious that their own agency was of the slightest importance to the work in which they were

engaged ; and yet they devoted themselves to their work
with as much zeal and earnestness as if they felt that the
result depended upon the personal efforts of each.   Adams,
Allen, Andrew, Howe, Mann, Palfrey, Parker, Phillips,
Sumner !

> ' Lives of great men all remind us
> We may make our lives sublime.'

When has been granted to one generation the inspiration
of such men ?   To the age which they lighted up and led,
they have left an imperishable record of ' noble ends by
noble means attained ; ' to us who knew and loved them,

> ' Learned their great language, caught their clear accents,
> Made them our patterns, to live or to die,'

they have left their great examples, precious memories, and
immortal hopes."

THE PRESIDENT : The Free Soil party of Massachusetts in 1848 was fortunate in its candidate for
governor, — Stephen C. Phillips, of Salem, distinguished for his earnestness, his unselfish devotion,
and the power with which in his addresses and writ-
ings he appealed to the Antislavery and " conscience " sentiment of the people of the State.   His
career was prematurely closed, or he would have
been called to high public service.   We pay our
tribute to him to-day, as we call upon his filial
representative, Stephen H. Phillips, at one time
Attorney-general of Massachusetts.

ADDRESS OF STEPHEN H. PHILLIPS.

MR. PRESIDENT, — I thank you most profoundly for the
affectionate tribute you have paid to one so near and dear
to me.   I have some memory of the stirring events of the

days when the Free Soil party was in its infancy, and some reminiscences may be recalled with interest. The first of many serious conversations with my father that I can remember in regard to the tendency of the times was in 1844. I was then just out of college, and just beginning the study of law ; and I remember one day in Salem, toward the close of the Clay campaign, that Judge Charles Allen, of Worcester, — a name never to be mentioned without respect in such an audience as this, — came down there and said to my father : " My name has been put on the electoral ticket of the State of Massachusetts, but I begin to think that Mr. Clay is playing us false. If it comes to that, I will stand out against the whole movement, Clay or no Clay, party or no party ; and I will vote against the ticket if there is to be any truckling to the slave power. It is abominable, and I will not submit to it ! "

I mention that to show the intense earnestness of feeling in those days. Looking back at it, I do not think it was true that Mr. Clay intended to play false; the alarm was in itself, I think, false, but the remark showed the intense individuality of Judge Allen. Well, Mr. Clay was defeated, but the electoral vote of Massachusetts was cast for him, and Judge Allen voted for him. Immediately afterward there began a movement on the Texas question, and it was at that time, I remember, that my father told me he had received a communication from Mr. Webster, which led up to the Free Soil conference, and on the whole subject both were very serious. Mr. Webster said : " This is a Gordian knot ; it cannot be dissevered, it must be cut." Shortly afterward, at Mr. Webster's suggestion, a meeting was called in Boston to protest against the annexation of Texas, and an address was prepared and sent out to the people of Massachusetts on the subject. That address was practically the work of Mr. Webster; and contains these words : " Annexation is calculated and designed, by the open declaration of its friends, to uphold the institution of slavery, extend its influence, and to cause its permanent duration." He took the pains to write this with his own pen. I hold the manuscript of that address in my hands. A large part of it is in Mr. Webster's handwriting, and all of it was written at his dictation. Well, that was after all the proposition, the energetic demand, of the Free Soil party.

Mr. Phillips here produced the original manuscript, written on large gilt-edged paper, such as was then supplied to senators and cabinet officers at Washington. He added that he always understood the address to have been prepared in Boston, at Mr. Webster's office, corner of Court and Tremont streets. Mr. Phillips then proceeded : —

The convention was held. Soon afterward a pamphlet was published, signed first by the name of "John Hampden," but afterward changed, at Mr. Webster's suggestion, to "A Massachusetts Freeman," which was widely circulated throughout Massachusetts, with Mr. Webster's approval. Things went on. We had struggle after struggle ; old friends deserted us and new friends came to our support, and the Conscience Whigs proceeded to organize themselves. My friend here on the right [Mr. Bird] is perhaps the only representative of that little body of men who used to meet for consultation and conference in Mr. Adams's office. Not one of those men wished to leave the Whig party, but they were forced by the inevitable tendency of things ; cost what it might, they had to do it, and do it they did. The organization was made, and from that time forth the die was cast and the work went on. That work is all before us, and the friends who are here to-day might well adopt the language of Macaulay, and say : "Its law has been progress. The point which yesterday was invisible is its goal to-day, and will be its starting point to-morrow." If there is anything which will cause any of us to take pride in those who have gone before, it is their devotion to the cause and their energy in its behalf.

Mr. Phillips spoke of the earnest warning given him by Anson Burlingame against leaving the Whig party when both were in the Law School together; and continued : —

But Mr. Burlingame lived to change his views. If there is any one experience strongly impressed upon my memory, it is a conversation with Mr. Burlingame, at Faneuil Hall, while the crowd were waiting for the arrival of speakers, and before the meeting was fairly opened, at which John Van Buren spoke. Calls were made for several different gentlemen, and Mr. Burlingame, who was sitting near me in a front seat in the gallery, was singled out as a promising young Whig politician who could not accept General Taylor, but whose standing had not become very clearly defined. He sprang forward in answer to the call, and his position was no longer uncertain. " We are standing," he said to his old Whig friends, " by the guns where you have posted us, and we mean to serve them." That was the introduction of Anson Burlingame to Free Soil politics in Massachusetts. Burlingame afterward became a strong supporter of the Free Soil movement. Robert Rantoul, Jr., was also spoken of as leading the forces in Essex County against slavery, and it was said that if he had lived, his voice would have been heard in higher places.

I think we have a right to look back with no ordinary pride at what has been accomplished by the Free Soil leaders. It is very easy now to meet in a warm and comfortable room and say, " We will pay a grateful tribute to their memory; " but when we think of what they did and of what they had to suffer, it is something for us to ponder over.

THE PRESIDENT: You will now listen to one — not old enough to vote in 1848, but coming of age a year or two later — who has probably addressed more audiences than any man now living in Massachusetts, — JOHN L. SWIFT.

ADDRESS OF GEN. JOHN L. SWIFT.

FOR half a century we have known the verse of our Free Soil poet, whose hands we have lovingly grasped to-day. Over and over again have we read that charming New England idyl, Whittier's " Snowbound." At the close he says : —

> " Haply, in some lull of life,
> Some Truce of God, which breaks its strife,
> The worldling's eyes shall gather dew,
> Dreaming in throngful city ways
> Of winter joys his boyhood knew ;
> And dear and early friends — the few
> Who yet remain — shall pause to view
> These Flemish pictures of old days."

In that spirit, we, old Free Soilers, in the sunset of our lives, sit around this table to look together upon the pictures of the past.

My words will be few, and from a lump that keeps coming up in my throat, it is doubtful if I get on smoothly, or a great way. Here once more are those who have not met for years, and yet for years were associated in a political movement compared with which nothing was ever braver in political morals or political contests. And looking into these faces, how it all comes back! Once more we see the crystallization of the youth of Massachusetts around that most splendid interpretation of American po-

litical duty, — free soil, free speech, free press, free men!
a crystallization beginning in its elementary force in that
trust in God where two or three were met together in the
name of liberty, to end in the tramp of two million armed
men and an inseparable nation, acknowledging no master
and knowing no slave under the flag. My first vote was a
Free Soil vote; my first memories are Free Soil memories;
my first warm friends of early manhood were Free Soil
friends. Whatever else has come to my heart of experience or change, there has never been anything but respect
and love for the " Old Guard," dead and living. All the
real estate I have, *unmortgaged*, is a burial lot at Forest
Hills. How soon I am to rest there I do not know, or
fear to know. I would not have the spot where I am to
be laid in the arms of Mother Earth designated with marble
or by comment cut in stone; but going by that green
mound, if those who outlive me halt for a moment and
say, " Here lies an old Free Soiler," they may see the grass
and the leaves bow their welcome to the words, and the
sunlight smile through the rifts of the foliage in response
to their greeting.

Standing here the past rises up before me. I am again
carrying a torch in one of those Free Soil processions that
always had in its earliest stages more torch-bearers than
votes. Again I am in Faneuil Hall, listening to Charles
Sumner as he lifts our thoughts on wings of eloquence to
the hallowed summit of the " higher law." Again we as-
sent to Henry Wilson, that man of the people, as he " ven-
tures to predict." Again with Anson Burlingame I pass
hours that run into days at the hospitable home of our
Nestor here, Hon. Francis W. Bird, — " Frank " was his
name in old Free Soil days; and one day as the grand
jury was in session to look after the seditious leaders in
the effort to rescue Anthony Burns, I remember he came
and invited me to go with him and Daniel Wells Alvord

fishing in the Adirondacks; he thought the air of that mountain region more conducive to the health and safety of a Free Soiler than the easterly winds of Boston: this was before that blessed tract had been desecrated by the trout romancer. Again I read "Warrington's" incomparable letters, — the brightest, wittiest, ablest correspondent of newspapers Massachusetts ever produced. Again I pace and repace Cambridge bridge, breathlessly listening, till after midnight, as Burlingame foreshadows that moment, — yes, that supreme moment in American history, — when it was found that there was a point where Americans reared in the free institutions of the North would risk their lives for honor or for principles, either by combat of two on the soil of Canada, or by armed legions on the soil of the South. Again I see the faces, and some are here to-day, of that faithful band who every year met the evening before the Free Soil State conventions, irrepressible and enthusiastic, and as faithful to these gatherings as the chosen race of Israel was faithful to feasts and to days when the tribes went up together. Then was shaped that bold, audacious, forward, unyielding American policy which became American destiny, and which lately, on the floor of Congress, from the lips of a generous Kentuckian, received the most magnificent burst of eloquence over Massachusetts' courageous leadership that ever has been or ever will be uttered.

Who of us can feel other than justifiable pride as we to one another recall these scenes, "all of which we saw, and part of which we were"? It has been said of our fathers that "they went to war against the trained armies of England with two field-pieces, a raw militia, and an idea." Like them we grappled with a trained, organized political force intrenched in every department of the nation, with a few conventions, a crude platform, and with raw recruits pledged to live or die by the idea that peace and order in this republic were impossible without equal and exact justice for all men, white or black. That grand and uncompromising idea linked the Free Soil ballot to the throne of the most high God. At last that glorious and irresistible idea under Abraham Lincoln became the reigning political thought; and by a victorious army overmastering obstacles that seemed insurmountable, and by processes almost miraculous, there was established the fact of free soil and the theory of free men and an unfettered speech and press on every foot of American territory.

To-day, without raising any questions of present duty, or lifting the veil upon the future, I bow before the mighty stride for human rights that has been made since we first rocked the Old Cradle of Liberty to Free Soil cheers and echoes. When Lafayette visited this country in 1824, he was received at a municipality in Connecticut on his way to Boston from New York. The chairman of the committee was an old Revolutionary soldier who had fought under Lafayette at Monmouth. He had not seen him for forty-five years, and he wondered if the brave General would recognize him. When they met, the captain from emotion could not speak. Lafayette looked at him, rushed to him, threw his arms about him, exclaiming, "Captain, my old comrade, God bless you!" My old Free Soil comrades, God bless you, every one!

THE PRESIDENT : We have a gentleman of accurate knowledge, acquired by experience as well as study, who can tell you how the Free Soil faith, once regarded as moral and political heresy at the South, has finally got a foothold in that region which was the seat of American slavery in 1848, but is now free. I refer to EDWARD ATKINSON, of Brookline, who will now address you.

ADDRESS OF EDWARD ATKINSON.

GENTLEMEN, — I cannot bring to you many reminiscences of 1848. I came of age in that year, and threw my first vote for the Free Soil ticket. I had, however, been in close relations as a youth with the old Whigs and the cotton manufacturers of that day, and this relation with the cotton industry has continued ever since.

The only incident that I can recall may show that the Devil is not always as black as he is painted. In the time of the old New England Emigrant Aid Society, of which I was one of the original stockholders, I applied to the Deacon of one of the Orthodox churches of Boston, an old Whig, for money with which to purchase Sharp's rifles to be sent to Kansas. " Oh," said he, " I can't give you any money *to buy guns with ; I can't do that ;* but see here, the men who carry the guns will need some beef, and I will give you twenty-five dollars to buy some beef for them." He gave me the money, and it went into the general fund. I never asked for a voucher to verify the beef purchase.

It has been said here to-night that *the theory* of free speech has extended throughout our land. I can myself bear witness not only to the theory but to *the fact* that free speech has extended throughout all the South. It was my fortune to be called upon to speak in the senate chamber of Georgia in October, 1880, upon the proposed Cotton Exposition, which they then desired to have established in Atlanta. I had a picked audience of sixty or seventy men, as many as the senate chamber could hold comfortably seated ; the Governor and the principal officials, one United States senator, ex-Senator Toombs, and many other leading men, politicians, merchants, and manufacturers were present. I had recently written an article on the

Solid South ; and a few days before I reached Atlanta an attack had been made upon me in one of the Southern papers by a clergyman who said that it was not fit that such a representative of the North should be called upon to speak to them. It was clear that there might be objection to my speaking, and I said to myself, Now is the time to try this question, and it shall be tried. I began in a quiet way, but before I had gone far in my address I said to them something like this : —

" Gentlemen of the South, I intend to use free speech for a purpose, and to speak plain words of truth and soberness unto you. I will not permit myself to insult you by admitting even in my own mind that I cannot speak my convictions and ask certain home questions here with as much independence as I can in my own little town in Massachusetts. If any one objects to free speech, let him do it now. Thank God, that time has gone by ! I speak to you here and now as a Republican of the Republicans, as an Abolitionist of early time, a Free Soiler of later date ; but I also speak, and yet more truly, as a Democrat of Democrats, because no man can be a true Democrat who does not maintain the equal right of every man, without distinction of race, color, or condition, to speak, act, and vote as he freely chooses."

Then and there I received as hearty a round of applause as I ever secured in any address I have ever made. A little later on I used these words : —

" There can be no general progress where the laborer is not worthy of his hire ; and that land will always be accursed where the man who earns his daily bread by the work of his own hands is not honored. When slavery ended, not only were blacks made free from the bondage imposed by others, but whites as well were redeemed from the bondage they had imposed upon themselves. In that dark and distant past did your cotton land improve in product every year ? Or, to quote the words of Henry A. Wise, of Virginia, ' Did not your niggers skin the land, and your white men skin the niggers ? ' To quote again from Dr. Cloud of Alabama, ' Did n't you gully your hillsides, and blast your prairies ? ' "

And then a little further on, quoting from the minister
who had attacked me, I said to them : —

"It has been said here within a few days that the Northern
forces two million strong, backed with all the wealth of the North,
had come down here *to subdue you.* It is not true. You have not
been subdued, either by Northern men or Northern wealth; you
have surrendered only TO THE PRINCIPLE OF LIBERTY which was
incorporated in the Constitution of the United States by your
ancestors as well as mine, — by Laurens of South Carolina and
Patrick Henry of Virginia, as well as by Hancock and Adams
of Massachusetts; and I call upon you to thank God with me
that you were not strong enough to break down that principle of
liberty."

Never before in all my life had I received such an ovation
of applause as I did then and there. And then I said to
them : —

"But I fear we have made a mistake. I witness the progress
that you are making in all the arts and industries born of liberty
in competition with us of the North. Suppose I go back, summon
again the armies and navies of the North to come down here two
million strong, backed with all our wealth, to put again upon your
shoulders the burden of slavery which you have thrown off, — you
would fight harder to keep it off than you did to maintain it; and
THEN you would beat us every time, and rightly, too. Thank God
again that the Potomac has not become the Rhine, dividing two
sections, with two hostile armies watching each other in camp and
barracks even in time of peace, burdening each section with the
evils of standing armies that are eating out the heart of foreign
countries ! "

Again came the hearty applause.

A few days later, sitting at the table with an ex-Confederate General of South Carolina, I tried my customary
method of seeing how far one might go in free speech.
I said : —

"One day at a meeting of the old Vigilance Committee in
Boston — "

He interrupted me, asking, "What was that?"

Said I, "A committee to rescue fugitive slaves."

"Oh," said he, "I never heard of that committee before."

I went on: "I was talking with Theodore Parker."

He interrupted me again: "Did *you* know Theodore Parker?"

"Oh, yes," said I, "he was one of my friends; I revered him."

Said he, "I wish I had known him; he was one of the greatest men this country ever produced."

I again resumed: "In conversation with Theodore Parker, he said to me, 'Mr. Atkinson, has it ever occurred to you that this condition of slavery *is a state of passive war*, and the only logical outcome of passive war *will be active war, by which it will destroy itself?*'"

"When did he say that?"

"Oh, in the fifties, just after the Fugitive Slave Law was passed."

"Well," said the General, "I told you just now that Theodore Parker was a great man; I always thought so, and now I know it. He was absolutely right. What he said was true."

A year later I again visited Atlanta. This time I had occasion to address an audience of a thousand or more persons. In that speech I stated to them that I expected to live to see the day when either the ex-Confederate soldiers or their children would erect a monument to John Brown upon the heights of Harper's Ferry in token of the emancipation which he had brought to the white men of the South. If you can find an example of free speech more complete than that, I wish you would. The suggestion was not received with applause, but neither did it excite any antagonism. After I had sat down, my old friend Mr. Asabel Smith, who had been Secretary of State in Texas when Sam Houston was President of the Lone Star State, came to me and said, "Mr. Atkinson, I go with you on every point save one." "That's the statue," said I. "Yes," said he, "I'm too old for that; perhaps you will live to see it, but *I* don't expect to." Now that seemed a rash prediction; yet not many months ago, the editor of the "Century Magazine" sent me a manuscript to revise, which was afterward printed, written by an ex-Confederate officer of high rank, now a professor in one of the Southern colleges, in which the ground was taken that the North itself had not witnessed the greatest benefit that had grown out of the war, and *that had been the emancipation of the white man of the South.*

Now, gentlemen, what more complete justification could be found for the Free Soilers of 1848 than these examples which I have given you of free speech upon the free soil of our Southern land? Or again, what more complete justification of the wisdom of our great war governor John A. Andrew, when he counselled us after the war still to move on with a "vigorous prosecution of peace"? Such has been the revolution not only of institutions but of ideas in our Southern land, and so fully have our Southern friends learned the lesson that the local self-government for which most of them claimed to fight was wholly inconsistent with the existence of slavery, — and yet more, so well has the lesson been learned that in their very defeat they have gained the cause of local self-government for which they fought, that there are none with whom we can join more heartily hand in hand to sustain the Union than the representatives of local self-government and State rights — not State sovereignty; there is a broad distinction — in South Carolina and in Massachusetts. Perverted no longer by the existence of slavery in their ideas of what State rights consist in, the men of the South and the men of the North may well unite in maintaining local self-government under the central sustaining power of this great nation, to which the allegiance of all is now so cheerfully and so fully rendered.

The President : Among the Free Soil speakers of 1850–1852 was John Winslow, of Newton. It was my privilege during those years when we were fellow law-students at Cambridge to listen to him, and on more than one occasion to speak with him from the same platform. Indeed, he gave me my first opportunity of the kind when we addressed the people of his village at the Upper Falls in that town in 1850. He has since attained a high place in his profession, and his name is found at the head of the best enterprises in his adopted city of Brooklyn, where at present he is president of the New England Society. I introduce to you Mr. Winslow.

ADDRESS OF HON. JOHN WINSLOW, OF BROOKLYN, N. Y.

Mr. Chairman and Gentlemen, — This is a charming commemoration of the Free Soil epoch, and naturally draws together the surviving, serious, thoughtful veterans who were active Free Soilers in Massachusetts in 1848. I am glad to be with you.

The Free Soil movement, though not confined to Massachusetts, was largely supported by her people. As we knew it in Massachusetts, we may recall such noble names among the leaders as Palfrey and Wilson and Sumner and Phillips and Jackson and Keyes and Burlingame and Allen and Adams, not to speak of the living, — names that will be respectfully remembered as long as the history of liberty shall be read and revered.

It is difficult to refer to any special circumstance or incident that led to the formation of the Free Soil party. It was called into existence by two great forces that came into irrepressible conflict. On the one side was slavery, aggressively asserting political right and power; on the

other side was that love of justice and freedom which God
has given to man. The history of the great fight can
be traced and identified by the opposition of the Free
Soilers to the teachings of John C. Calhoun, who was the
able defender of slavery and of its right to dominate all
public policy that could possibly affect or impinge upon the
barbarism called the "institution of slavery." Calhoun
believed that the "institution" could not live if Antislavery ideas and agitation were not suppressed. Abraham
Lincoln, in later time, said the same thing in his own way,
when he declared the country could not remain half slave
and half free.

In 1828, when the tariff bill was pending in Congress,
Calhoun, as the leader of the free-traders, found himself
opposed by Van Buren and Jackson. Calhoun was determined, as he said, to bring the protective system to an
end. This led him to assert the sovereignty of the States,
and he was soon found pushing the doctrine to extremes.
He invoked the Virginia and Kentucky resolutions of
1798-99, and expounded the doctrine of nullification, —
the right of each State to prevent within her limits the
enforcement of such Acts of Congress as she might con-
sider unconstitutional. In 1828 Calhoun set forth this doctrine in an elaborate paper, which came to be known as
the "South Carolina Exposition." This led later to the
famous debate in the Senate between Senator Hayne, of
South Carolina, and Daniel Webster. Here let me say,
Mr. Chairman, that whatever criticisms may be justly made
upon the course of Mr. Webster in his later years, touching
the aggressions of the slave power, the great principles
he advocated in that masterly speech for the conservation
of Liberty and Union, — an advocacy that has not its equal
in the annals of American statesmanship in breadth and
depth and lucidity of statement, — were the principles that
inspired our people in the final struggle *vi et armis*, and

gave victory for the Union as the preserver of constitutional freedom.

We find Calhoun struggling to stem the Antislavery tide by marshalling the State-sovereignty theories to the defence of slavery. One of his measures was a bill in the Senate, subjecting to severe penalties any postmaster who should knowingly receive and put into the mail any publication or picture touching the subject of slavery, to go into any State or territory in which the circulation of such picture or publication should be forbidden by the State laws. The report asserted the doctrine that the States were sovereign as to one another, bound together only by compact. In his speech Calhoun made an alarming statement of the numbers and zeal of the Abolitionists, and of the danger of their discussions and principles to the South. He also insisted that all petitions for the abolition of slavery in the territories and the District of Columbia ought to be rejected altogether, because Congress had no jurisdiction over the subject. This denial of the right of petition was ably and stoutly contested by John Quincy Adams in the House on many occasions.

In a letter written in 1847 to a member of the Alabama legislature, Mr. Calhoun declared that he was from the beginning in favor of " forcing," as he expressed it, the slavery issue on the North, believing that delay was dangerous, and that the South was relatively stronger, both morally and politically, than she would ever be again. Calhoun repeatedly in the course of the Senate debates declared his conviction that slavery was a positive " political and social good." He said that Randolph was right in opposing the Missouri Compromise, and that if the Southern members had acted and voted in the spirit of Mr. Randolph, abolition might have been crushed forever in the bud. In March, 1844, Tyler called Calhoun to his cabinet to continue a negotiation begun by Upshur for the annexation of Texas.

Mr. Webster had been ejected from the office of Secretary
of State to make a vacancy for Upshur. Upon Upshur's
death Calhoun renewed the effort.

Mr. Calhoun combated the Wilmot Proviso, and introduced resolutions in the Senate taking extreme ground in
denying the right of Congress to legislate against slavery
in the territories. Soon after General Taylor's election,
Calhoun called together some eighty Southern members of
Congress, and as chairman of a committee reported an
address, which was signed by forty-eight senators and representatives. It denied the power of Congress to exclude
slavery from California and the other new territories, and
even denied the power of the legislature or the inhabitants
of the territories to exclude it. The South was urged to
hold no connection with any party at the North not prepared to enforce the Constitutional guarantees in favor of
the South. Among the neglects or refusals of the North
to do this, the failure to enforce the old fugitive-slave
law was named and vehemently denounced. And so to
the end of his life Calhoun was the defender of slavery and
of its political claims and aggressions. Most of the political thought in the Free Soil days, whose memories we
recall with so much interest here to-day, turned therefore
upon the propositions maintained or opposed by John C.
Calhoun touching the great barbarism.

I have thus given you, Mr. Chairman and Gentlemen,
some of the reasons for my view that the history of the
Free Soil controversy is largely identified, in opposition,
with the positions taken by Calhoun upon the great issue.
Calhoun was the profound thinker of the South. In the
Free Soil days and before, Joshua Leavitt, the able editor,
debater, and writer, was constantly attacking slavery, and
especially the positions taken by Calhoun. It is said that
Calhoun pronounced Mr. Leavitt to be the ablest and most
dangerous adversary of slavery in the country.

In the year 1846, when the breach was more apparent than before in Massachusetts between the " conscience " and the " cotton " Whigs, the former had hopes that both Choate and Webster would soon become identified with them. In this chapter of political history there was a memorable day in Faneuil Hall, in September, when I was present as a spectator, and which may properly be referred to here as illustrative of the political atmosphere of the period. The Whig State Convention was in session, and many leading men of both sides were there. The contest was as to the platform, whether it should be conservative or of an Anti-slavery type. Before it was reported, Sumner made a speech of great power and eloquence in favor of aggressive action against the usurpation of the slave power. In his speech he made a graceful and forcible appeal to Mr. Webster, saying : " Dedicate, sir, the golden years of experience which are yet in store for you to removing from your country its greatest evil. In this cause you shall find inspirations to eloquence higher than any you have yet confessed." Winthrop was then called out and made an able reply. There were two sets of resolutions reported, as was expected. Speeches were made by J. Thomas Stevenson and Linus Child on the conservative side, and by Stephen C. Phillips, Charles Francis Adams, and Charles Allen on the Antislavery side. The debate was able, attended by much excitement, and lasted until night. The conservatives became alarmed, and decided to send for Webster. Joseph Bell, chairman of the Whig State Central Committee, soon appeared, with Webster upon his arm, amid tremendous applause. Both " conscience " and " cotton " Whigs joined in manifestations of respect. As Webster reached the rostrum, the applause was renewed with great vigor, and the whole scene was grand and inspiring. Webster took his seat and listened to Charles Allen, one of the ablest of the " conscience " men, who resumed and finished a stern and inflexible speech. Webster then rose, the convention rising with him, and in a short address made a plea of great power for harmony. A friend tells me that Sumner said he knew, when he saw "Black Dan" coming, it was all up with his side that year. It was in this speech that Webster's famous words were uttered which have been so widely quoted. He had been speaking of his warm attachment to the Whig party, and how he loved to inhale its "odor of liberty." Then followed the memorable words spoken in his grandest and most impressive manner. "Others," he said, "rely on other foundations and other hopes for the welfare of the country; but for my part, in the dark and troubled night that is on us, I see no star above the horizon promising light to guide us but the intelligent, patriotic, united Whig party of the United States." At this moment every look and gesture of the orator were in harmony with his thought. He seemed to speak as if standing in a dark background, his lustrous eyes looking above the horizon for the star that should give the promised light to guide the convention and the people. The power of the speech and the spectacle was seen and felt in the fact that a convention of turbulent men, at once subdued, were ready for adjournment without further strife.

In Massachusetts the men who worked together as Free Soilers generally co-operated in the Coalition movement that brought about the election of Governor Boutwell, in 1851, and of Senator Sumner. You and I, sir, Mr. Chairman, took some part, as young men, in that struggle under the direction of the State Committee. We addressed the people in many towns, and found it good to be in the thick of the fight. We were room-mates at Cambridge Law School at the time, and learned in that experience what it was to meet young men students from the South, who differed from us on the great subject, and who seasoned their expressions of dissent with that peppery condiment peculiar to the Southern temperament. In those days our Southern friends sincerely believed that one of their good men would prove equal to any three of ours in combat, and in that spirit they argued and protested. That this spirit was somewhat modified, if not entirely removed, by the battles of the Civil War is quite likely true.

The Free Soilers encountered no little opposition from many of the elderly men holding high positions in the churches, such as Rev. Dr. Nehemiah Adams and Prof. Moses Stuart. As illustrative of this, let me tell you of an interesting incident at Andover, then largely under the influence of Prof. Moses Stuart, distinguished for his stubborn conservatism and stiff opposition to the abolitionists, as the Free Soilers were sometimes called when disrespect was intended.

It was in the campaign of 1848, when the late Richard H. Dana was expected to address the Free Soilers one evening in a village church at Andover. Many of us who were then members of Phillips Academy attended, and were disappointed at the non-arrival of the distinguished speaker. There was a large audience, including a number of the theological students. Professor Stuart was living in Andover at that time, and continued to maintain his aggressive opposition to the Free Soil movement. When it became apparent that for some reason Mr. Dana would not be with us, there were persistent calls upon several of the " theologs " to speak ; but none could be induced to respond. Those of us of pronounced Free Soil views were inclined to think that the gentlemen thus called upon had the fear of the mighty Stuart upon them ; at any rate, no gentleman of the seminary would speak. It seemed a pity to send the audience away without the desired instruction, and the boys and young men of the academy began to call upon such of their number as were

7

known to be acceptable speakers. At first there was a
modest hesitancy; and to get the ball rolling I told two
of our fellow-students, the late lieutenant-governor of New
York, Hon. William Dorsheimer, and Mr. John K. Valen-
tine, who for many years has held the office of United
States District Attorney in Philadelphia, that if they would
agree to speak, I would lead off. You may imagine the
apparent relief of the audience upon our appearance. We
got along pretty well, and I may assure you we did not spare
the enemy. The applause was tumultuous and hearty;
but whether the people most liked our pluck or our manner
of putting things, we never knew. If any of you have any
knowledge of the solemn, earnest nature of the late Rev.
Samuel H. Taylor, the principal of Phillips Academy at
Andover at that time, you will not be surprised to hear
that the next morning, when he found us hoarse, and not
prepared in Greek (his favorite study), we were severally
invited " to remain " after recitation. He expressed grief
at our conduct, and told us of the dangerous influence of
political excitement as an interruption of study. I took
him into my confidence at once, and told him we agreed
with him fully, and that such an occasion would never come
again, and that he might rest in peace. It never did come
again ; but we enjoyed the satisfaction of knowing that we
saved and possibly instructed the meeting, and were not
deterred in our performance of duty by the presence in
the town of the learned professor whose ponderous influence we knew was against the Free Soilers.

Standing here to-day in this presence, I look back, as I
know you do, Gentlemen, to the days of the Free Soil
campaign with no feeling of regret, but rather of joy, that
you and I were permitted to take some part for a sacred
cause that at last triumphed, in the most absolute sense.
We resisted the encroachments of the dominant slave
power, and have lived to see the four millions of slaves

who were its victims become freemen; and also have
lived to see, as a necessary sequence, the Constitution so
amended as to be in fact an instrument of freedom in all
our land. So now we live, in a truer sense than before, in
the " land of the free and the home of the brave."

THE PRESIDENT: Who of us does not delight to
recall Erastus Hopkins, of Northampton, his attrac-
tive presence on the platform, his grace and power
as a speaker, and his continued service while he
lived for the Antislavery cause ? He is with us not
only in memory, but in the person of his son, Col.
W. S. B. HOPKINS, to whom you will next listen.

ADDRESS OF COL. W. S. B. HOPKINS.

MR. CHAIRMAN, — The compliment you pay to my dear
father by including me among the survivors of the Free
Soil party of 1848, recognizing in me a title to the honor
by right of representation, is very kind and very grateful to
me. In 1848 I was an enthusiastic boy politician of twelve
years, drinking in and assimilating with my developing
nature the lofty principles that were then brought to the
front, never again to be relegated to the rear in the minds
and consciences of the American people. I am conscious
how deeply the lessons of that day became seated in me,
not only for their own moral and political importance, but
by reason of earnest parental instruction, met, I will dare
to think, by a proper filial reverence.

Born to work at a later day, I nevertheless was in some
ways so associated with the political status and with the
growth of the idea of the non-extension of slavery from
1848 to the election of Lincoln, that to me as well as to some
of you who are older everything political which has occurred
since — save only the political aspect of the war — seems

dwarfed and selfish in comparison. Free soil in all the new States and the public domain, which was the *demand* of the men of 1848, was *achieved* in the election of Lincoln. The step beyond that — free soil throughout the land — was the *consequence* of the slave-holders' war. The re-establishment of a lasting and giant republic on the firm basis of recognized and conceded nationality was the product of all three.

You who are here to-day, and those who were then associated with you and who are gone to rest, were the pioneers in this great political revolution which washed the nation clean from her disease, and gave her that sturdy health which assures a vigorous and useful life. In the sequel there have been times when some have become heartsick and distrustful, as early leaders often do; but the fruit of the seed you sowed has nourished a people who, however divided into parties and on policy, are a people of sublime faith, marching to a sublime destiny.

I have said you were pioneers. But you did not, like the pushing men who have carried the flag westward, lay out your work in the free wilds where you had an unfettered sweep and unchallenged control. You fought your early battles surrounded by men native to the soil as well as you, in whose breasts were rooted all the timid conservatism, all the prejudice, and all the selfish partisanship which poor weak human nature draws in with mother's milk, and develops and petrifies by custom. Thus you challenged, received, and bravely bore contumely and savage attack inflicted by neighbors and friends. The weapon of ostracism was resorted to, and personal enmities, for a time at least, sundered established ties of friendship. In saying this I am not citing what I have learned in political history only. I bear personal testimony; for when a boy, with tingling ears I heard my father berated in a public meeting at Northampton, by two eminent lawyers up to that moment his friends, for his devotion to principle, in language suited only to the traitor and turncoat who deserved the whipping-post if not the gallows.

But it is meet that these trials to which you were subjected should be, as they have been, nearly forgotten and quite forgiven. This gracious duty has been the easier because of the success of your cause. Persecution could not make you martyrs, though it may have made you heroes. It is your proud prerogative to see your patient persistence in putting principle before the American conscience rewarded, not with the martyr's crown, but, thank God! with the victor's laurel. Such men are born for leaders while they live ; and in every advance of the great cause of progress since their first stand for the right, the men of 1848 *have* led, and while they live *must* lead, in enlightened thought and high purpose.

Again I thank you for the privilege of drawing new inspiration from this re-union.

THE PRESIDENT : We give a hearty welcome to HORACE E. SMITH, now Dean of the Law School at Albany, N. Y., who in Free Soil days was living in Chelsea in this State, the partner of Henry B. Stanton, and who, in association with Mr. Bird, was one of the managers of "The Free Soiler," our campaign paper in 1851.

ADDRESS OF HON. HORACE E. SMITH.

MR. CHAIRMAN, — I came here to listen and enjoy, not to speak ; and I feel now that my silence would contribute more to the pleasure of the company than my speech. I should continue to decline your kind and repeated invitation to say a few words, but for the fear that my silence might be mistaken for indifference. No language at my command

is adequate to express my interest in this reunion. When
I look around upon men who were prominent in the movement which we here commemorate, the animus, action, and
scope of which have been so eloquently portrayed in the
speeches to which we have listened, and memories of the
stirring events that ensued spring up within me, I seem to
hear a voice saying, " Put off thy shoes from off thy feet;
for the place whereon thou standest is holy ground."

You have intimated, Mr. Chairman, that no minor strain
should mingle in our communion and congratulations on
this occasion. I cannot, however, forbear a passing reference to distinguished leaders in the struggle for Free Soil
who have passed beyond the river, and whose familiar faces
we miss in this gathering. We who are " alive and remain
unto this day " cherish their memory with deep tenderness
and great respect. With but a slight change in a passage
of sacred Scripture, we might appropriately apply to them
the beatitude, " Blessed are the dead which die in the cause
of freedom from henceforth : Yea, saith the Spirit, that
they may rest from their labors ; and their works do follow
them."

These men, our fallen comrades, do rest from their earnest, self-sacrificing labors ; and their noble works do follow
them in a rich harvest of blessings. As I was compar-
atively young when the Free Soil party was organized, and
inconspicuous in the early struggle against the extension of
slavery, I think I may say without any violation of propri-
ety that in my judgment we are indebted to the ability,
devotion, and firmness of the Free Soilers for the integrity
of the Federal Union and the blessings of freedom enjoyed
by a great and prosperous nation. The priceless treasure
of a free nation with a republican government, secured and
established by our fathers, and defended, cemented, and
strengthened by their children, we may now reasonably
hope to transmit unimpaired to future generations. We

have listened with much pleasure to a speech from the son of that noble man and eminent leader Erastus Hopkins, whom I well knew, and to whose marked ability and single-ness of purpose I take pleasure in bearing testimony. Referring to the early Antislavery movement, the speaker said in substance that the men of that day were born for the struggle. This reminded me of an incident in General Grant's tour around the world, which may be familiar to all present. While in Pekin, on the occasion of a demonstration by the Government in his honor, the premier essayed to address him in English; and wishing to compliment the General with the *original* remark that he was "born to command," expressed himself thus: "Sire, great generale, you vas made to order." I think, Mr. Chairman, that the leaders in the Free Soil party were "made to order."

I will only add that it is one of the most gratifying reflections of my life that I was permitted to bear an humble part in the great struggle for freedom and human rights which we to-day so auspiciously commemorate. By this communion I feel stronger for whatever remains to me of duty in the future.

Thanking you, Mr. Chairman, for your courtesy, and expressing my gratitude for the privilege of enjoying this intensely interesting occasion, I will say farewell.

THE PRESIDENT: The Free Soil party of Massachusetts found its greatest strength, in 1848, in the sturdy patriotism of the city and county of Worcester, under the leadership of Charles Allen. The Whig party in that section, until that time its stronghold, was reduced to a hopeless minority. We have with us several gentlemen who did good service there, and they will address you,—JOHN C. WYMAN,

now of Valley Falls, R. I.; Thomas Drew, now of
Newton; and Albert Tolman and Henry H.
Chamberlain, then, as now, citizens of Worcester.

ADDRESS OF JOHN C. WYMAN.

Mr. President, — I feel that it is good to be here; but
I am surprised at being called upon at this time, and I can
truly say that I am as unprepared as I am surprised. There
are so many about me who were influential and distinguished in the inauguration of that great political revolution known as the Free Soil movement, who have not
yet spoken, that it seems to me it would be a much wiser
disposition of the time to have them improve it, since I
can merely occupy it.

I confess, sir, that while I distinctly remember that I
was one of the young men in Worcester, in 1848, who were
somewhat active in politics, and in hearty sympathy with
the bold and courageous action of our delegate, Hon.
Charles Allen, to the Whig National Convention, in repu-
diating the nominations and the platform of the party,
I have forgotten many of the details. I am indebted to
my friend Thomas Drew, one of the veterans of the Worcester press, who was even then in active service, for the
information that I was one of a committee of twenty-
six, chosen at a meeting of Free Soilers in Worcester,
to make arrangements for the great mass convention in
that city, June 28, 1848, the fortieth anniversary of
which we commemorate to-day. In looking over the list
which my friend has shown me, I am reminded how ruth-
less and relentless is the scythe of Time. Of the whole
number only ten survive; and as evidence of the tena-
cious fidelity with which the old Free Soiler clings to
principle, and cherishes the precious memories of that
grand uprising of the people of Massachusetts forty years

ago, I wish to state that four of the ten — Messrs. Albert Tolman, George W. Russell, William A. Wallace, and myself — are here to-day.

No one unfamiliar with the conditions then existing in the politics of the time can realize the magnitude — nay, the hopelessness — of the task which the Free Soilers of that day assumed. There was intense excitement all over the land. Texas had been annexed, new territories were soon to be organized and admitted into the Union as States, and the slaveholders had boldly avowed their purpose to make of them slave States. Here and there a protesting voice was heard from men of both the great political parties; but the leaders of opinion were timid and compromising, fearing to lose electoral votes in the South if a decided stand should be taken to thwart the designs of the slave power. Thus it happened that the Whig national convention nominated General Taylor for the presidency, who was a large slaveholder; and a few weeks later the Democrats nominated General Cass, whose views upon the slavery question were considered not unfriendly to the South.

In the Whig convention at which General Taylor was nominated, an effort was made to secure a plank in the platform providing that slavery should be prohibited in the territories; but it was derisively hooted down. Then it was that Judge Allen came forward, and in behalf of his constituents threw down the gauntlet of defiance. His action was bravely seconded, as you know, by Henry Wilson. They came home, and in the old town hall of Worcester Judge Allen gave an account of his stewardship. It was a magnificent meeting, — one which those present will never forget, for it was plainly evident that the people approved his conduct and would heartily sustain him. Most fortunate it was for us and for the cause of freedom that we had for a leader a man of such unwavering fidelity,

8

such persistent courage, and such matchless ability as advocate and orator. In eloquent and scathing terms he showed the cowardice and treachery of the leaders of both parties, especially his own. He portrayed the disasters that would befall the republic if the schemes of the slave power, as already developed, were not thwarted at once; and he appealed to his fellow-citizens to stand steadfast for the right, as their forefathers had done. The heart of that great county was thrilled by his appeal, and the response of the people came in a unanimous resolve to labor early and late in support of " Freedom, Free Soil, Free Speech, a Free Press, and a Free Land." Thus did the great work begin.

The lesson taught by the example of Judge Allen, Mr. Sumner, Mr. Wilson, Stephen C. Phillips, Charles Francis Adams, J. G. Palfrey, F. W. Bird, Horace Mann, Dr. S. G. Howe, and all the others who were active in the great movement in those eventful days, is, I think, that fearless fidelity to principle always finds its reward in ultimate success. These men sought not and cared not for office. Freedom, as a principle and a right, not as a privilege, was the demand they made upon the conscience of the country; and how grand has been the result! Some of them did not live to see the fruition of their hopes; but we who are here to-day can bear grateful testimony to the purity of their motives and the grandeur of the results of their actions.

Emerson has somewhere said that " the standard of civilization is not determined by the census, by the large cities, nor by the crops, but by the MEN which a country produces." Measured in this way, who can estimate the value of the work begun by the men who were founders of the Free Soil party? They saw the country dominated by the slave power, holding four million human beings as chattels, and eager to strengthen, enlarge, and perpetuate that domination by any methods, even to the destruction of all the ancient landmarks, and the subversion of all the principles of civil liberty upon which the government was founded.   Behold the result! Within the boundaries of the republic there exists not a single slave ; and even the desire to possess one has ceased forever among our brethren of the South.   The Mason and Dixon line has lost its old significance as a boundary between Slavery and Freedom. The vast territories of the West and Southwest, then in dispute, have become sovereign States, and are already dotted all over with towns and cities where race distinctions are not recognized and all are equal before the law.

Surely, we old Free Soilers, in reviewing the past and contrasting what *was* with what *is*, cannot fail on an occasion like this to find ourselves in full sympathy with Whittier's beautiful lines, —

> " Yet who, thus looking backward o'er his years,
> Feels not his eyelids wet with grateful tears,
>   If he hath been
> Permitted, weak and sinful as he was,
> To cheer and aid, in some ennobling cause,
>   His fellow-men ? "

Mr. THOMAS DREW of Newton was introduced as the only survivor of the Free Soil editors of Massachusetts in 1848.   He was associate editor with Elihu Burritt (the Learned Blacksmith) of the " Christian Citizen " at the time the convention was held ; and from 1849 to 1859 he was also one of the editors and proprietors of the Worcester Daily and Weekly " Spy," whose senior editor, John Milton Earle, did faithful work for the Antislavery cause many years before the Free Soil party was organized.

In responding, Mr. DREW prefaced his remarks as follows : —

ADDRESS OF THOMAS DREW.

In one of the fables of Æsop we are told that upon the defeat of an army in battle a trumpeter was taken prisoner. The soldiers were about to put him to death when he said, " Nay! gentlemen, why should you kill me? This hand of mine is guiltless of a single life." " Yes," replied the soldiers, " but with that brazen instrument of yours you incite others, and must share the same fate." I can give both the fable and its moral a personal application; for it was my good fortune to act the part of trumpeter to the gathering hosts of freedom, with an instrument which if less brazen than the one used by Æsop's trumpeter was not less efficient, and perhaps better suited to the times; namely, the printing press.

To illustrate his position in aid of the cause whose grand success they had met to celebrate, Mr. DREW read the closing paragraph of an editorial from the " Christian Citizen " of June 24, 1848, written by himself in the absence of the editor-in-chief Elihu Burritt, who was in Europe. He said that the " Call " for the first Free Soil State Convention in Massachusetts did not seem to him, at the time, quite forcible enough for the occasion; and in giving it gratuitous insertion in the " Citizen," he supplemented it as follows : —

Come, then, men of New England, to the rescue! Come from the dense rich forests and fertile river-sides of Maine! Come, ye stalwart dwellers among the granite ridges of New Hampshire, and ye who breathe the pure air of freedom in Vermont! Come, ye of Connecticut and Rhode Island! Leave for a time your workshops and your fields, your spindles and your looms, and unite with the men of Massachusetts, who are rallying from every section of the State to make an effort for freedom worthy of her cause. Come! for you will hear words of wisdom that will make you strong. You can listen to the eloquence of him who in the First Congress was the most powerful advocate of the Declaration of Independence speaking in his grandchild's voice. You will hear, too, the burning words of him who upon the anniversary of the nation's birth first ventured to point to the people a truer meed of glory than that which comes from successful conquests and deeds of blood. You will hear, too, from the man who was kicked out of South Carolina by that sovereign State for making the simple demand for a trial by jury for our own citizens, when unjustly and unconstitutionally confined in the prisons of Charleston for no other crime than the color of their skins. Others, too, of the great and good will be present to address you upon the need of resistance to the exactions of the slave power. Let there be no lack of numbers or enthusiasm; and let the voice of New England echo back the swelling notes of freedom that are borne to us upon every western breeze from great meetings of the people, to give the world assurance that although their leaders have betrayed them, the people still scorn to be slaves!

ADDRESS OF HENRY H. CHAMBERLAIN.

Mr. President, — The few remarks which I shall offer on this occasion will be confined to some recollections of the first Free Soil movement in Worcester, and of Hon. Charles Allen's connection therewith.

It will be remembered that the eighth representative district of Massachusetts chose as delegate to the Whig convention in Philadelphia in 1848 the Hon. Charles Allen. He went there expecting that Mr. Webster would be the nominee of the party as candidate for the presidency; but hardly had he arrived when he learned to his dismay and indignation that the nomination of General Taylor had been agreed upon, and that the North was to be appeased by the nomination of Mr. Abbott Lawrence for the vice-presidency.

Mr. Allen, thus early informed of this arrangement, was prepared to meet it; and when the nomination was confirmed by vote of the convention on the third ballot, he arose in his place and denounced the proceedings, saying, " As the Whig party of the North are not to be allowed to fill with their statesmen any offices of trust, therefore we declare the Whig party of the Union is this day dissolved." He further said that " he would not be bound by the proceedings of the convention;" and amid cries of " turn him out," " sit down," etc., he foretold that Massachusetts would " spurn the bribe," and turning his back on the assembly he left the hall to return no more.

When the news of Mr. Allen's course reached Worcester there was great commotion among his constituents, and curses loud and deep were hurled upon his devoted head. Notwithstanding all the objurgations cast upon Mr. Allen, there were a few persons who quietly expressed their approbation of his course; and it was agreed that I should see him upon his arrival home and ask him to address his constituents. I accordingly did so. He replied, "If you think there will be any persons to hear me, I will gladly address them. Who will come to the meeting? I don't care to speak to empty benches; but if you think we can fill a small hall, I will go and speak." The next day we began to hear of a few persons who were favorably inclined, and would go to hear him, and we decided that it was safe to hire a "small hall" and advertise that Mr. Allen would address his constituents. On the following day we found "the woods were full of them," and we were encouraged to engage the largest hall in town, to notify Mr. Allen of what we had done, and to call a public meeting.

The hour for the meeting having arrived, the self-appointed managers assembled at the hall to find it crowded to its fullest capacity; even the windows were filled, and every "coign of vantage" was occupied. The meeting was called to order by Mr. Oliver Harrington, and Mr. Albert Tolman was chosen to preside, while I was despatched to escort Mr. Allen to the hall. By much crowding we were enabled to reach the platform, where he was introduced to the assembly, and made that great speech which proved to be the death-knell of the Whig party in Massachusetts. In the course of his speech Mr. Allen made this statement: "When I said the Whig party was dissolved, I but declared a fact. It is dead. The undertakers may preserve its corpse for a little while, but it will soon become offensive to the smell and the sight, and must be removed from the sight of the people." At the close of Mr. Allen's speech, Hon. Henry Wilson, who was in the hall, made a short address, after which appropriate resolutions were passed.

Just as the assembly were about to retire, Rev. George Allen appeared on the platform, and offered the following resolution, which was received with great enthusiasm and unanimously adopted : —

"*Resolved*, That Massachusetts wears no chains and spurns all bribes ; that Massachusetts goes now and will ever go for Free Soil and Free Men, for Free Lips and a Free Press, for a Free Land and a Free World."

THE PRESIDENT : There is a time for all things, and the time has now come to bring this commemorative occasion to a close. It has been to all of us, I trust, one of glad reunion and of pleasant memories.

Several gentlemen having expressed a desire that a report of the proceedings should be published in pamphlet form, the matter was referred with full powers to a committee consisting of Hon. MILO HILDRETH of Northborough, JOHN A. NOWELL of Boston, and HENRY O. HILDRETH of Dedham. The subject of calling future reunions of the Free Soilers of Massachusetts was also referred to the same committee.

On motion of Hon. STEPHEN H. PHILLIPS, of Salem, a vote of thanks to the presiding officer was unanimously passed, and at six o'clock the meeting was dissolved.

APPENDIX.

———◆———

CALEB A. WALL, for years connected with the "Worcester Spy," and an active participant in the stirring scenes of 1848, had prepared a speech giving interesting reminiscences concerning the early meetings held at Worcester, which was crowded out of the proceedings by want of time. The following abstract from Mr. WALL's speech will be read with interest: —

REMARKS OF CALEB A. WALL.

SOON after the Whig and Democratic Presidential nominations of 1848 became known, six or seven persons in Worcester, five of whom are present at this gathering to-day, — Albert Tolman, Henry H. Chamberlain, George W. Russell. John C. Wyman, and William A. Wallace, — well representing the dominant political feeling of the time there in reference to those nominations, were specially instrumental in organizing that sentiment into action ; and it found its first public expression in a meeting at the City Hall, Wednesday evening, June 21, at which Mr. Tolman presided, and Mr. Wallace, then foreman in the "Spy" office, was Secretary. The full proceedings of this meeting, including the masterly two hours' speech of Judge Allen, are contained in the "Daily Spy" of June 23, 1848.

At this meeting. which was called to hear Judge Allen and to take the initiatory steps for the organization of the new party, a committee of twenty-six well known citizens of Worcester — ten of whom are now living, and five of the number are present at this Reunion — was chosen to make the necessary arrangements for the holding of the first Free Soil State Convention at the same place, the following week, June 28, 1848, when the party was formally organized. The ten persons of this committee of arrangements now living are Albert Tolman, Henry H. Chamberlain, James F. Allen, John C. Newton, Benjamin E. Hutchinson, Peregrine B. Gilbert, Samuel Davis, and Thomas A. Clark, all still of Worcester; John C. Wyman of Rhode Island, and William A. Wallace of East Canaan, N. H. The members of this committee who have deceased were Charles Allen, Alexander DeWitt, Charles Washburn, Oliver Harrington, Rufus D. Dunbar, Edward Hamilton, Edward H. Hemenway, Joseph Boyden, Enoch Hall, Dr. H. G. Darling, Joseph A. Gilbert, Albert P. Ware, Charles Hadwen, Augustus Tucker, and Edward Southwick.

General Wilson, coming in while Judge Allen was speaking, was greeted with enthusiastic applause, and followed the Judge in remarks in support of their course. After the regular resolutions of the meeting sustaining their action had been reported and adopted, Rev. George Allen, a brother of the Judge, who had been detained by his duties as Chaplain at the State Hospital, came in, and offered impromptu that remarkable resolution which afterwards became so famous. "*Resolved*, That Massachusetts wears no chains and spurns all bribes; that Massachusetts goes now, and will ever go, for free soil and free men, for free lips and a free press, for a free land and a free world." This sentiment was received with so much favor that the author of it was requested to commit it to writing, which he did, after which it was adopted with unbounded enthusiasm, and subsequently passed at various meetings and conventions during that campaign, including the Massachusetts State Convention held the following week at the same place; the main sentiment of the resolution was incorporated in the platform of the National Free Soil Convention held in August following at Buffalo, where Martin Van Buren and Charles Francis Adams were nominated for President and Vice-President of the United States, and its leading doctrine, embodied in every subsequent national Republican platform, has since become a part of the Constitution of the United States.

At the State convention of June 28, at the Worcester City Hall, where the Free Soil party was ushered into existence in due form, all sections of the Commonwealth were represented, and large numbers were also present from other States, filling the hall at an early hour to its utmost capacity. The convention was called to order at 10 A. M. by Hon. Alexander DeWitt of Oxford, and organized temporarily by the choice of Hon. S. F. Lyman of Northampton as chairman, and William S. Robinson [Warrington] of Lowell as Secretary. A committee consisting of Edward L. Keyes of Dedham, John S. Eldridge of Boston, William Bassett of Lynn, H. G. Blaisdell of Lawrence, J. W. Brown of Framingham, Augustus Tucker of Worcester, William H. Stoddard of Northampton, and John H. Morse of Sherburne. was then chosen to nominate a list of permanent officers of the convention, which they did, as follows, and these were unanimously elected: President, Hon. Samuel Hoar of Concord; Vice Presidents, Alanson Hamilton of West Brookfield, Hon. Joseph L. Richardson of Medway, Dr. Samuel G. Howe of Boston, John Wells of Chicopee, Joseph Stevens of Warwick, Richard P. Waters of Salem; Secretaries, William S. Robinson of Lowell, William A. Wallace of Worcester, Allen Shepard of Ashland, William A. Arnold of Northampton.

The proceedings were opened with prayer by Rev. George P. Smith, then pastor of the Old South Church. On taking the chair, the President, Hon. Samuel Hoar. was greeted with great applause, reference at his introduction to the vast audience being made to his treatment by the officials of South Carolina, while there as the agent of Massachusetts for the protection of colored citizens from this State who had been outrageously deprived of their Constitutional rights while in South Carolina on legitimate business. After remarks from the Chair, on motion of Hon. Stephen C. Phillips of Salem, a committee to draft an address and resolutions was chosen, consisting of Stephen C. Phillips, Erastus Hopkins of Northampton, Daniel W. Alvord of Greenfield, Milton M. Fisher of Medway, Allen Bangs of Springfield, William B. Spooner of Boston, John Milton Earle of Worcester, and E. Rockwood Hoar of Concord. On motion of Samuel F. Lyman of Northampton, a committee to nominate a State Central Committee was chosen, consisting of S. F. Lyman, Alexander DeWitt, E. R. Hoar, F. W. Bird of Walpole, Albert Tolman of Worcester, and Ebenezer Lamson of Shelburne; and this committee subsequently reported the names of the following gentlemen, who were unani-

mously elected as State Central Committee, to have charge of the
State campaign work, — Hon. Charles Francis Adams and George
Newcomb of Quincy, S. F. Lyman of Northampton, Dr. Caleb
Swan of Easton, Allen Bangs of Springfield, Henry Wilson of
Natick, Edward L. Keyes of Dedham, Milton M. Fisher and John
P. Jones of Medway, George Minot of Reading, William Bassett
of Lynn, Freeman Walker of North Brookfield, Alexander De-
Witt of Oxford, and Henry T. Parker of Boston. This committee
organized for subsequent action by the choice of Edward L. Keyes
as Chairman, and William Bassett as Secretary.

The mass delegations from Boston and other sections of the
State were received with great cheering as they entered the hall,
which soon became so crowded that an adjournment to the Common became necessary, to hear the speaking. After the transac-
tion of the preliminary business, John S. Eldridge of Boston read
a letter from a mass meeting holding in Philadelphia, addressed
to this convention, expressive of enthusiastic confidence in the
final triumph of the great revolution for liberty then going on all
over the land. Stephen C. Phillips read a resolution of thanks to
Charles Allen and Henry Wilson in endorsement of their course
in repudiation of the nominations at Philadelphia. Judge Allen
was then introduced amid great applause, and made an able address in support of his action, which was enthusiastically received.
Charles Sumner read a letter from Hon. J. R. Williams, M. C., a
delegate to the Philadelphia Convention from Michigan, in sympathy with the objects of this convention. Addresses followed
by Henry Wilson, the coadjutor of Judge Allen at Philadelphia,
Abram Payne of Providence, R. I., John C. Woodman of Maine,
Amasa Walker of North Brookfield, Joshua Leavitt of Boston,
Lewis D. Campbell, M. C., of Ohio, and others, strongly approving
the objects of the gathering.

The afternoon session of the convention was held in what was
called " Hospital Grove," on the south side of the lot where now
stands the State Normal School. At the opening, Hon. Stephen
C. Phillips, chairman of the committee on address and resolutions, made an elaborate and ably written report, which he read
in his well-remembered eloquent manner, his powerful voice making itself distinctly heard throughout that vast assembly, amid
frequent applause. With what emphasis did Mr. Phillips read

this expressive resolution: " That Massachusetts looks to Daniel Webster to declare to the Senate and to uphold before the country the policy of the Free States; that she is relieved to know that he has not endorsed the nomination of General Taylor; and that she invokes him, at this crisis, to turn a deaf ear to 'optimists' and 'quietists,' and to speak and act as his heart and his great mind shall lead him"!

At the beginning of this significant reference to the great Massachusetts statesman the speaker was interrupted with "No! No!" from several voices in different sections of the audience ; but on Mr. Phillips explaining that the resolution only said " looks to Daniel Webster," with strong hopes that he might on this question be true to his highest declarations in the past, without expression of confidence that he would do so, the objectors were satisfied, and the address and resolutions were adopted entire.

With what enthusiastic cheering was the following resolution of the series received, when read by Mr. Phillips : " That the following language of Henry Clay, which has often been echoed by the Whig party, is a rebuke of that same party for its nomination of General Taylor : ' If, indeed (said Mr. Clay) we have incurred the divine displeasure, and if it be necessary to chastise this people with a rod of vengeance, I would humbly prostrate myself before God, and implore Him in His mercy to visit our favored land with war, with pestilence, with famine, with any other scourge than military rule, or a blind and heedless enthusiasm for mere military renown'"! The force of this resolution is seen in the fact that General Taylor was nominated purely on account of his successful leadership in a war which had been pronounced by the Whigs of the Northern States "the most infamous war ever waged in all human history."

Among the other resolutions was one endorsing the course of Senator John P. Hale of New Hampshire and Representative Joshua R. Giddings of Ohio, in Congress : eloquent speeches followed by Mr. Giddings, Charles Francis Adams, Charles Sumner, E. Rockwood Hoar, and others, and the following delegates at large were chosen to the National Free Soil Convention held at Buffalo, N. Y., August 9 and 10, — Stephen C. Phillips of Salem, Daniel W. Alvord of Greenfield, William Jackson of Newton, John M. Brewster of Pittsfield, Charles B. Sedgwick of Stock-

bridge, and John A. Bolles of Boston ; with thirty district delegates including such representative men as Charles Francis Adams,
Richard H. Dana, Jr., John B. Alley of Lynn, Joshua Leavitt of
the " Boston Emancipator," David Lee Child of Boston, Gershom
B. Weston of Duxbury, John Mills of Springfield, George F.
Farley of Groton, Chauncy L. Knapp of Lowell, Nathan Brooks
of Concord, Albert G. Browne of Salem, Alexander DeWitt, Rho-
dolphus B. Hubbard, Charles White of Worcester, and others.

Hon. MILTON M. FISHER, of Medway, was called upon by
the President, but he had left the room in consequence of
sudden indisposition. The following is an abstract of the
remarks he had prepared for the occasion : —

REMARKS OF HON. MILTON M. FISHER.

MR. PRESIDENT, I assume that it is simply from the fact that I
am providentially the only one of two representatives now living,
and the only one present to-day of fifteen members of the Committee on Resolutions adopted at the organization of the Free Soil
party, that I am asked to say a word on this occasion. In the
more vivid remembrance of that eventful day, and the progress
marked by it in the great Antislavery movement, beginning nearly
twenty years before, I had well nigh forgotten my incidental relation to it, until your announcement of the fact in your opening
address.

Everything has a beginning ; the Free Soil party was not an
exception. But something always precedes a beginning, and
something preceded the Free Soil party, else it had never been.
Antislavery sentiments — convictions held with the tenacity of a
divine inspiration — preceded it. They found early utterance in
Garrison and Whittier, Lovejoy and Leavitt, Quincy and Phillips,
through the " Liberator " and the " Emancipator," and many pul-
pits. They were crystallized as a moral sentiment in the American
Antislavery Society in 1833, and politically in the Liberty party
in 1840. The latter organization was hopeful and aspiring, if not
vigorous and stalwart, when the Free Soil party was organized.
Yes, Mr. Chairman, it had a vitality in the conscience and intelli-

gence of the people that could not have been annihilated, but as
Joshua Leavitt said at the Buffalo Convention in August, 1848,
might be, as it was, "translated" bodily into a wider realm of
immortality through the Free Soil party of the Republic.

It was my honor and privilege, with Charles Francis Adams of
Quincy (a conscience Whig) and William J. Reynolds of Roxbury (a barnburner Democrat), to represent the Liberty party
of Norfolk County in that first National Convention of the Free
Soil party which augmented the rising tide still higher, until,
through the Republican party of 1856, — by the pen of Abraham
Lincoln, — the armies of the Union, and "the gracious favor of
Almighty God" the death-struggle of a generation ended in victory for " FREE SOIL, FREE LABOR, and FREE MEN."

Yes, Mr. Chairman, the men and the women too who talked
and prayed in schoolhouses and chapels, who worked till towns
and counties were roused and organized for aggressive and efficient
service, are entitled to high credit and honorable mention on this
occasion as the pioneers and heralds of the Free Soil party.
Among them were the saints and martyrs of the gospel of
Liberty who suffered death and the loss of all things for the cause.
Few escaped a social and political ostracism and the scorn and
contempt of former friends, equivalent to death itself; and some of
us are old enough to know whereof we speak.

But, Mr. Chairman, the former things have passed away. If it
were not a day for reminiscences we might indulge in anticipations.
It is enough for us that our lives and deeds are a matter of history,
and that God in his providence has vindicated the cause we es-
poused. For the future we need not fear. The old Roman proverb
is still our hope and trust, — "Magna est veritas et prævalebit."

Hon. ALBERT TOLMAN made a brief address mainly in
review of the early vote of the party in Worcester, but
with characteristic modesty declined to prepare a report
for the press, for the reason assigned that the work would
be better done by his friends from Worcester.

LETTERS.

AMONG the letters received are the following: —

LETTER FROM DR. BOWDITCH.

BOSTON, June 7, 1888.

MR. HENRY O. HILDRETH.

DEAR SIR, — It would afford me sincere pleasure to join the survivors of those who formed the Free Soil party, but circumstances beyond my control will prevent me from so doing. I was a " Liberty Party " man when it polled only twenty votes in Boston; therefore I feel that I could rightfully take my seat among the *Juniors*, because I was one of the " Old Guard " and in a warm fight for Liberty before some of your Free Soilers were born into the noble contest.

I wish that your meeting may be, and I have no doubt that it will be, an entire success.

Respectfully yours,   HENRY I. BOWDITCH.

LETTER FROM JOHN G. WHITTIER.

DANVERS, June 27, 1888.

HON. WILLIAM CLAFLIN.

MY DEAR FRIEND, — I am not in a condition to " dine out," but if my health admits, I shall try and look in upon you at Parker's for a few minutes and shake hands with my old friends of 1848. We are all justly proud of the record of the party we formed forty years ago. It saved the Union; it abolished slavery. If it has made some mistakes incidental to fallible humanity, it has been and still is faithful to its original doctrines of human equality and the free exercise of the rights of citizenship, irrespective of color or condition. It has never gone back on the Declaration of Independence. We have good reason for rejoicing over its past, and in the prospects of its future success and usefulness. Hoping to see thee to-morrow, I am

Always thy friend,   JOHN G. WHITTIER.

LETTER FROM SENATOR HOAR.

UNITED STATES SENATE,
WASHINGTON, D. C. Aug. 21, 1888.

HENRY O. HILDRETH, Esq.

MY DEAR SIR, — I do not think it will be in my power, without subjecting your publication to an inconvenient delay, to give the contribution to it which you ask. I hope at some early day, when I have time, to make some pretty elaborate contribution to the political history of that period.

I am yours very truly,

GEO. F. HOAR.

LETTER FROM JUDGE HOAR.

CONCORD, Sept. 1, 1888.

HENRY O. HILDRETH, Esq.

DEAR SIR, — I have been absent from Massachusetts the past month, which has caused the delay in receiving and replying to your kind note of August 20.

I am glad to hear that the proceedings of the Reunion of Free Soilers held in Boston in June last are to be preserved in pamphlet form, and shall hope to be able to procure a copy.

As reported in the newspapers, they were extremely interesting to me, especially the address of E. L. Pierce, who presided, and I much regretted that it was out of my power to be present. But age and infirmities have so far unfitted me for participation in public meetings, that it is very doubtful whether I should have said anything if I had been there; and what, if anything, I should have said, I fear is beyond human wit to determine.

The men who were there assembled had been large contributors to their country's welfare, and it will always be a source of great satisfaction to me that I was able to lend a hand in such a work, and with such associates.

Very truly yours,

E. R. HOAR.

THE FREE SOILERS OF 1848 AND 1852.

In the " Boston Commonwealth " of March 7 and May 9, 1885,
there were printed lists of more than one hundred of the prominent Free Soilers of 1848 and 1852, prepared by Hon. EDWARD
L. PIERCE. These lists, which were mainly confined to the Free
Soilers of Eastern Massachusetts, are reprinted here, with such
additions as could be conveniently made, as a partial record of the
members of that historical party. The most prominent leaders
are grouped together, and the other names are simply arranged in
alphabetical order. There has been no attempt at completeness,
many being omitted who were quite as worthy to be mentioned as
others who are included.

Since the organization of the Free Soil party in 1848, there
have been three conspicuous social gatherings of the members in
Massachusetts, — the banquet given to Hon. JOHN P. HALE, in
the hall of the Fitchburg Railroad·Station in Boston, May 5, 1853,
at which fifteen hundred Free Soil men and women were present ;
the dinner given by the late SAMUEL DOWNER, at Downer's Landing, Hingham, August 9, 1877, that being the 29th anniversary
of the Buffalo Convention, which was attended by two hundred
gentlemen ; and the Reunion, to the proceedings of which this vol-
ume is mainly devoted.

CHARLES FRANCIS ADAMS, born in Quincy, Aug. 18, 1807; died
in Boston, Nov. 2, 1886. From 1815 to 1848 he did perhaps more
than any one, by his contributions to the Boston " Whig " which he
conducted, by his addresses and his wise counsels, to consolidate the
Antislavery section of the Whig party; and from 1848 to 1852 he
continued active in speaking, and also contributed considerable sums
for the promotion of the cause.

CHARLES ALLEN, of Worcester, born Aug. 9, 1797; died Aug. 6, 1869.
More than any one after the Whig National Convention in 1848,
in which he declared his determination to oppose General Taylor's
election, he brought the heart of the Commonwealth to the support of

the Free Soil cause. In character he is worthy to be placed by the side of Samuel Adams.

John G. Palfrey, of Cambridge, born May 2, 1795; died April 26, 1881. His papers on the "Slave Power," growing out of the annexation of Texas, and his popular addresses, were very effective.

Stephen C. Phillips, of Salem, born Nov. 1, 1801; died June 26, 1857, by the burning on the St. Lawrence of a steamer on which he was a passenger. He was a gallant leader of the Antislavery section of the Whig party, both as writer and speaker, and his evident sincerity and earnest eloquence were very impressive in his popular addresses. His sons, Stephen H. and Willard P., both still living, were in entire sympathy with him.

Charles Sumner, of Boston, born Jan. 6, 1811; died in Washington, as Senator, March 11, 1874. He was the coadjutor of Mr. Phillips and Mr. Adams from 1845, both by speeches and in contributions to the newspapers.

Henry Wilson, of Natick, born Feb. 16, 1812; died in Washington, as Vice-President, Nov. 22, 1875. He was the most indefatigable of all the Free Soilers, made more addresses, wrote more articles, and knew more men in the party than any other leader. He organized and inspired the coalition which overthrew the Whigs, having in this movement the sympathy and co-operation of Sumner, but not of Phillips, Adams, or Palfrey.

———

Shubael P. Adams, born Feb. 5, 1817; formerly of Lowell, but now living in Dubuque, Iowa; active as a writer and speaker in the years of 1848–1853.

Daniel Allen, of Walpole, died Jan. 22, 1880, aged sixty-five.

John B. Alley, of Lynn, born Jan 7, 1817. The coadjutor of Wilson and Bird in organizing the Free Soil movement.

John A. Andrew, of Boston, born May 31, 1818; died Oct. 30, 1867. His speeches were marked with ability and fervor, and his office at No. 4 Court Street was the starting-point of effective work for the cause.

Edmund Anthony, of New Bedford, born Aug. 2, 1808; died Jan. 24, 1876.

Daniel W. Alvord, of Greenfield, born Oct. 21, 1816; died Aug. 3, 1871, in Fairfax County, Virginia. Organized the Free Soilers of Franklin County.

Edward Atkinson, born in Brookline Feb. 10, 1827.

John D. Baldwin, of Boston and Worcester, born September, 1809; died June, 1883. Came from Connecticut to edit the " Daily Commonwealth " in January, 1853.

George M. Baker, of Marshfield, born in 1820.

Allen Bangs, of Springfield, born July 26, 1819; died Nov. 24, 1853.

John N. Barbour, of Cambridge, born in Boston, Oct. 4, 1805.

Samuel D. Bardwell, of Shelburne Falls, born May, 1819.

Francis W. Bird, of Walpole, born in Dedham, Oct. 22, 1809, was active and able as a writer and as an organizer of the Antislavery sentiment both in his county and in the State generally.

John A. Bolles, of Winchester, born April 16, 1809; died May, 1878, in Washington City.

Matthew Bolles, of Boston, born June 11, 1807.

Thomas T. Bouvé, of Boston, born Jan. 14, 1815.

Samuel A. B. Bragg, of Boston, born Nov. 2, 1825.

George M. Brooks, of Concord, born July 26, 1824.

Albert G. Browne, of Salem, born Dec. 8, 1805; died Oct. 10, 1885.

Anson Burlingame, of Cambridge, born Nov. 14, 1820; died in St. Petersburg, in the service of the Emperor of China, Feb. 23, 1870. He was always welcome as a speaker, particularly on account of the sentiment and enthusiasm of his speeches, qualities which were the product of his birth and early life in the West.

Joseph T. Buckingham, of Cambridge, born Dec. 21, 1779; died April 11, 1861. An incorruptible editor, who was forced to leave the " Boston Courier " because he was a " Conscience " Whig and refused to support Taylor in 1848. He was afterward a coalition Senator from Middlesex County.

Sanford Carroll, of Dedham, born in Walpole, Oct. 22, 1810.

Josiah H. Carter, of Dorchester, born Feb. 22, 1812.

Robert Carter, of Cambridge, born Feb. 5, 1819; died in New York, Feb. 15, 1879.

Otis Cary, of Foxborough, born June 14, 1804; died April 25, 1888.

George N. Cate, of Marlborough, born Dec. 11, 1824.

Francis Childs, of Charlestown, born July 20, 1820; an early organizer for John G. Palfrey's election to Congress. Died April 6, 1887.

Asaph Churchill, of Dorchester, born in Milton, April 20, 1814.

Joseph M. Churchill, of Milton, born April 29, 1821; died March 23, 1886.

Charles M. S. Churchill, of Milton, born May 1, 1825.

William Claflin, of Newton, born in Hopkinton, March 6, 1818.

Ebenezer Clapp, of Dorchester, born April 24, 1809; died June 12, 1881.

James Freeman Clarke, of Boston, died June 8, 1888, aged seventy-eight.

Asa Clement, of Dracut, born May 18, 1813.

Frederick Crafts, of Dorchester, died April 20, 1874, aged seventy-seven.

Joshua E. Crane, of Bridgewater, born July 9, 1823; died Aug. 5, 1888.

Richard H. Dana, Jr., of Cambridge, born Aug. 1, 1815; died Jan. 6, 1882, in Rome, Italy, where he is buried. A brilliant writer and speaker, and conspicuous for his services in behalf of fugitive slaves.

Charles G. Davis, of Plymouth, born May 30, 1820.

Robert T. Davis, of Fall River, born Aug. 28, 1823.

William T. Davis, of Plymouth, born March 3, 1822.

Alexander DeWitt, of Oxford, born April 2, 1798; died Jan. 13, 1879.

Samuel Downer, of Dorchester, born March 8, 1807; died Sept. 20, 1881. He gathered the Free Soilers at Downer's Landing in 1877.

Thomas Drew, of Worcester, born in Plymouth, Aug. 23, 1819. For many years identified with the Worcester "Spy."

John Milton Earle, of Worcester, born April 13, 1794; died Feb. 8, 1874. Editor of the Worcester "Spy."

Morton Eddy, of Bridgewater, born 1797; died in Fall River, March 24, 1888. He was one of two in Bridgewater who voted for Birney in 1840.

John S. Eldridge, of Canton, born Sept. 23, 1819; died March 23, 1876.

Charles Endicott, of Canton, born October 28, 1822.

William Endicott, Jr., of Boston, born in Beverly, Jan. 4, 1826.

Charles M. Ellis, of Roxbury, born December, 1818; died in Brookline, Jan. 23, 1878. A defender of fugitive slaves.

Alonzo H. Evans, of Everett, born in Allentown, N. H., Feb. 20, 1824.

MILTON M. FISHER, of Medway, born in Franklin, Jan. 30, 1811.

RODNEY FRENCH, of New Bedford, born May 2, 1802; died April 30, 1882.

GEORGE FROST, of Roxbury, born Dec. 11, 1819; died March 22, 1876.

THOMAS GAFFIELD, born in Boston, Jan. 14, 1825.

EBENEZER F. GAY, of Dedham, died Nov. 15, 1871, aged fifty-one.

GEORGE W. GAY, of Sharon, born in Roxbury, April 30, 1817.

TIMOTHY GILBERT, of Boston, born Jan. 5, 1797; died July 19, 1865. In a public card he defied the Fugitive Slave Act, and gave unwearied service to the cause.

DANIEL W. GOOCH, of Melrose, born Jan. 8, 1820.

FRANCIS R. GOURGAS, of Concord, died July 12, 1853, aged forty-two, while serving in the Constitutional convention.

JOHN GOVE, of Boston, born July 31, 1800; died May 14, 1871.

JOHN Q. A. GRIFFIN, of Charlestown, born July 8, 1826; died in 1866. Remarkable for his vigor of style and wit.

HENRY GUILD, of Boston, born in Dedham, Nov. 29, 1818.

CHRISTOPHER A. HACK, of Taunton, born Dec. 9, 1806.

NATHANIEL HALL, of Dorchester, born in Medford, Aug. 13, 1805; died October 21, 1875.

LEWIS HAYDEN, of Boston, born Dec. 3, 1811. A faithful colored servant to his brethren in bonds.

JOSEPH K. HAYES, of Boston, born Feb. 15, 1813. Resigned from the Boston police rather than aid in the return of a fugitive slave.

CHARLES A. HEWINS, of West Roxbury, born in Dedham, Jan. 4, 1822.

THOMAS WENTWORTH HIGGINSON, of Cambridge, born Dec. 22, 1823. An earnest worker and speaker.

HENRY O. HILDRETH, of Dedham, born in Dorchester, March 22, 1826.

MILO HILDRETH, of Northborough, born in Townsend, Aug. 17, 1824.

RICHARD HILDRETH, of Boston, born in Sterling, June 28, 1807; died in Florence, Italy, July 11, 1865. Noted as an historian and a political writer.

SAMUEL HOAR, born in Lincoln, May 18, 1788; died in Concord, Nov. 2, 1856. A man of marked character, and of great influence, especially in Middlesex County.

E. ROCKWOOD HOAR, born in Concord, Feb. 21, 1816. He was prominent as a "Conscience Whig," and active as a Free Soiler in 1848.

GEORGE FRISBIE HOAR, born in Concord, Aug. 29, 1826. He was too young to be very prominent in 1848, but he took a leading part in the Legislature of 1852, making an Antislavery speech.

ELI W. HOLBROOK, of West Boylston, born Dec. 22, 1809.

ERASTUS HOPKINS, of Northampton, born at Hadley, April 7, 1810; died Jan. 9, 1872.

APPLETON HOWE, of Weymouth, born Nov. 2, 1792; died Oct. 10, 1870.

ESTES HOWE, of Cambridge, born July 13, 1814; died Jan. 12, 1887.

SAMUEL G. HOWE, of Boston, born Nov. 10, 1801; died Jan. 9, 1876.

HENRY HUMPHREYS, of Dorchester, born April 3, 1801.

ATHERTON N. HUNT, of Weymouth, died Jan. 8, 1865, aged sixty-two.

CHARLES P. HUNTINGTON, of Northampton, born May 24, 1802; died Jan. 28, 1868.

WILLIAM JACKSON, of Newton, born Sept. 6, 1783; died Feb. 27, 1855.

EDWARD JARVIS, of Dorchester, born in Concord, Jan. 9, 1803 ; died Oct. 31, 1884.

JOHN P. JEWETT, of Boston, born Aug. 16, 1814; died May 14, 1884.

W. H. S. JORDAN, of Boston, born 1814.

JOHN A. KASSON, of New Bedford, born Jan. 11, 1822; now living in Iowa.

EDWARD L. KEYES, of Dedham, born in 1812; died June 6, 1859. He was an orator endowed by nature with remarkable powers, and both as editor and speaker was distinguished by his severe and trenchant style.

FRANKLIN KING, of Dorchester, born in Chesterfield, Dec. 8, 1808.

THOMAS KINGSBURY, of Needham, died May 14, 1859, aged sixty-four.

CHAUNCY L. KNAPP, of Lowell, born in Berlin, Vermont, Feb. 26, 1809.

PHILO LEACH, of Bridgewater, died Sept. 8, 1853, aged fifty-six.

JOSHUA LEAVITT, of Boston, born Sept. 8, 1794; died in Brooklyn, N. Y., Jan. 16, 1873. The well known Antislavery editor.

JOSEPH LYMAN, of Boston, born Aug. 17, 1812; died Aug. 14, 1871.

HORACE MANN, of Newton, born May 4, 1796; died in Yellow Springs, Ohio, as President of Antioch College, Aug. 2, 1859.

SETH MANN, of Randolph, born Feb. 28, 1817.

JOHN J. MAY, of Dorchester, born Oct. 15, 1813.

ANDREW McPHAIL, Jr., of Boston, born Feb. 28, 1817.

ANNIS MERRILL, of Boston, born in Harwich, Sept. 9. 1810. For many years a resident of California.

JOHN J. MERRILL, of Roxbury, born April 16, 1821.

JAMES H. MORTON, of Springfield, died in 1876, aged about fifty-three.

MARCUS MORTON, of Taunton, born Dec. 19, 1784; died Feb. 6, 1864. Acted with the Free Soilers in 1848, but later was more in sympathy with the Democratic party.

MARCUS MORTON, Jr., of Andover, born April 8, 1819. Now chief-justice of the State.

NATHANIEL MORTON, of Taunton, died in 1856, aged about thirty-seven.

ALVA MORRISON, of Braintree, born May 13, 1806; died May 28, 1879.

BENJAMIN B. MUSSEY, of Boston, born April 28, 1804; died Jan. 12, 1857.

CURTIS C. NICHOLS, of Cambridge, born in Freetown, March 6, 1814.

JOHN A. NOWELL, of Boston, born in Sandford, Me., May 16, 1817.

THEODORE OTIS, of Roxbury, born Dec. 15, 1810; died July 11, 1873.

JOHN C. PARK, of Boston, born June 10, 1804.

THEODORE PARKER, of Boston, born Aug. 24, 1810; died in Florence, Italy, May 10, 1860. Full of courage and forecast, and profoundly in earnest.

EDWIN PATCH, of Lynn, born May 12, 1820.

CHARLES A. PHELPS, of Boston, born Oct. 19, 1820.

WILLIAM PHILLIPS, of Lynn, born April 29, 1799.

EDWARD L. PIERCE, of Milton, born March 29, 1829. Active as a writer and speaker from early manhood.

HENRY L. PIERCE, of Dorchester, born Aug. 23, 1825. Active as an organizer.

JOHN PIERPONT. of Medford, born April 6, 1785; died Aug. 27, 1866.

HIRAM A. PRATT. of Easton, born August 12, 1826.

LABAN PRATT, of Dorchester, born in Weymouth, Nov. 15, 1829.

NATHAN B. PRESCOTT, of Roxbury, born 1827.

JOHN M. READ, of Boston, born April 1, 1809.

WILLIAM RICHARDSON, of Dorchester, died June 6, 1856, aged forty-two; remarkable for his personal influence and power in conversation and attracting his townsmen to the Free Soil movement at its beginning.

JAMES T. ROBINSON, of North Adams, born Sept. 6, 1822.

WILLIAM S. ROBINSON, of Lowell, born Dec. 7, 1818; died in Malden, March 11, 1876. A voluminous writer for the cause.

THOMAS RUSSELL, of Boston, born Sept. 26, 1825; died Feb. 9, 1887.

SAMUEL E. SEWALL, of Melrose, born Nov. 9, 1799. Now living as the Nestor of the Massachusetts bar.

THOMAS SHERWIN, of Dedham, died July 23, 1869, aged seventy.

JOHN SHOREY, of Dedham, born in South Berwick, Maine, 1804; died Sept. 4, 1849.

CHARLES W. SLACK, of Boston, born Feb. 21, 1825; died April 11, 1885. An early writer and speaker for the cause, and editor of the Weekly "Commonwealth" from October, 1864, to the time of his death.

HORACE E. SMITH, of Chelsea, now Dean of the Albany, N. Y. Law School. Born in Weston, Vt., Jan. 30, 1817. Active with voice and pen.

WILLIAM B. SPOONER, of Boston, born April 20, 1806; died Oct. 28, 1880. A generous friend of the cause.

GEORGE L. STEARNS, of Medford, born Jan. 8, 1809; died April 9, 1867. The friend of John Brown; rendered important service in raising colored troops during the Civil War, and in sustaining Antislavery newspapers.

CHARLES A. STEVENS, of Ware, born Aug. 9, 1816.

ELIPHALET STONE, of Dedham, born May 12, 1813; died Feb. 5, 1886.

JAMES M. STONE, of Charlestown, born Aug. 13, 1817; died Dec. 19, 1880. Did effective work in that locality.

JAMES W. STONE, of Boston, born Oct. 26, 1824; died Aug. 21, 1863. Active in organizing and collecting funds.

EBEN F. STONE, of Newburyport, born Aug. 3, 1822. Rendered efficient service in Essex County.

CALEB SWAN, of Easton, born 1796; died 1870. Addressed meetings in Bristol, Norfolk, and Plymouth counties, and was energetic in organizing the movement in his part of the State.

JOHN L. SWIFT, of Boston, born May 28, 1828. A most effective orator.

VELOROUS TAFT, of Upton, born Dec. 16, 1819.

JOSEPH B. THAXTER, of Hingham, born June 1, 1818.

ABIJAH W. THAYER, of Northampton, born Jan. 6, 1796; died April 24, 1864.

ADIN THAYER, of Worcester, born in Mendon, Dec. 5, 1828; died Aug. 4, 1888.

ELI THAYER, of Worcester, born June 11, 1819. Organizer of free state emigration to Kansas.

EDWIN THOMPSON, of East Walpole, born July 23, 1809; died May 22, 1888.

ALBERT TOLMAN, of Worcester, born Dec. 23, 1808. An untiring worker in the cause.

MARTIN TORREY, of Foxborough, died Nov. 2, 1861, aged seventy-two.

WILLIAM B. TRASK, of Dorchester, born Nov. 25, 1812.

SAMPSON R. URBINO, of Roxbury, born in Germany, April 18, 1818.

THOMAS L. WAKEFIELD, of Dedham, born June 15, 1817; died June 21, 1888.

EDWIN WALDEN, of Lynn, born Nov. 25, 1818.

WILLIAM A. WALLACE, of Worcester, born Sept. 28, 1815.

AMASA WALKER, of North Brookfield, born May 4, 1799; died Oct. 29, 1875.

OLIVER WARNER, of Northampton, born April 17, 1818; died September, 1885.

RICHARD P. WATERS, of Beverly, born Sept. 29, 1808; died May 19, 1887.

SETH WEBB, Jr., of Boston, born Feb. 14, 1823; died Aug. 31, 1862.

JOHN G. WEBSTER, of Boston, born April 8, 1811; died Feb. 7, 1886.

GERSHOM B. WESTON, of Duxbury, born in 1800; died in 1870.

John W. Wetherell, of Worcester, born July 16, 1820.

Henry B. Wheelwright, of Taunton, born May 24, 1824.

Nathaniel H. Whiting, of East Marshfield, born Nov. 24, 1808. An effective speaker.

William A. White, of Watertown, born Sept. 2, 1818; died in Madison, Wis., Oct. 10, 1856. An earnest writer and speaker.

Benjamin F. White, of Weymouth, died April 16, 1885, aged sixty-eight.

John G. Whittier, of Amesbury, born Dec. 17, 1807. Poet and writer for the cause, now living at Danvers, and still citizen of Amesbury.

Dudley Williams, of West Roxbury, born August, 1808; died March 6, 1888.

Franklin Williams, of Roxbury, born March 2, 1822; died Oct. 2, 1880.

John Winslow, of Newton, born Oct. 24, 1825. A speaker for the cause in 1850–1852, and now a lawyer in Brooklyn, N. Y.

William H. Wood, of Middleborough, born Oct. 24, 1811; died March 30, 1883.

Elizur Wright, of Boston, born Feb. 12, 1804; died Nov. 21, 1885. An early speaker and constant writer.

Stephen C. Wrightington, of Fall River, born Feb. 15, 1828.

John C. Wyman, of Worcester, born in Northboro', Sept. 13, 1822.

James M. W. Yerrington, of Chelsea, born October, 1825. An accurate reporter of Antislavery speeches.

REUNION OF THE FREE SOILERS OF FRANKLIN COUNTY.

THE following abridged report of the proceedings of the Franklin County survivors of the Free Soil party of 1848, which took place at Greenfield, Mass., Aug. 9, 1888, being the fortieth anniversary of the meeting of the Buffalo Convention, is taken from the " Greenfield Gazette and Courier."

In obedience to the call which had been issued, the Franklin County survivors of the Free Soil party of 1848 met at the Mansion House on Thursday, for a reunion and celebration. They came from nearly every town in the county, and with wives and daughters made a company of nearly fifty, which included many of the representative men of this vicinity. The following is the Secretary's list of those present, recorded by towns : —

Ashfield, H. S. Ranney; Bernardston, Rev. S. Barber, Joel N. Dewey; Buckland, R. W. Field, Frederick Forbes, George D. Crittenden, Dr. Josiah Trow; Charlemont, Warren Albee, J. N. Blodgett; Conway, L. S. Abell, S. Bradford; Deerfield, James Childs, A. W. Bates; Gill, J. B. Marble, A. E. Deane; Greenfield, Hopkins Woods, M. E. Darling, H. A. Potter, Rev. Dr. John F. Moors, J. Johnson, Sumner Chapman, T. M. Spicer; Heath, C. P. Coates; Leverett, Cephas Porter; Montague, Joseph Clapp, R. N. Oakman, Sr., Austin Drake; New Salem, Samuel H. Stowell; Northfield, A. C. Parsons, Addison Johnson, Charles Pomeroy; Shelburne, Samuel D. Bardwell, G. W. Mirick, D. A. Fisk, L. T. Covell; Shutesbury, E. G. Wood; Sunderland, K. Hubbard, S. D. Crocker, G. W. Graves, D. D. Whitmore.

An hour or two was spent in a social way, and in renewing old acquaintance. Dinner was served at one, after which the company assembled in the parlors to listen to the speeches which were characterized by the old-time fire and enthusiasm. R. W. Field, of Buckland, chairman of the committee of arrangements, called the meeting to order, and introducing the president of the day, said : —

" Forty years ago to-day a noble band of men met at Buffalo, and declared although both of the two great political parties had held their presidential convention and solemnly pledged and bound themselves that slavery was Constitutional and must not be agitated, 'This Buffalo Convention declares in the words of Patrick Henry, "Give me liberty, or give me death;" "Thus far and no farther, and here shall thy proud waves be stayed." Come weal or woe, no act of ours, no vote of ours shall uphold this accursed institution, and this is our proclamation. Not one foot more of free territory shall be given up to slavery.' You little thought then at Buffalo on the 9th day of August, 1848, and at the polls the coming November, that you had struck a blow that caused the chains of four millions of human beings to fall off, and that they were to become free and equal citizens of this great republic. The germ planted at Buffalo took root, and it was the beginning of the political party that placed Abraham Lincoln in the presidential chair, and it was reserved for his pen to sign the proclamation that slavery was in the past, no more to curse this country and invite the deserved judgment of heaven on this our beloved land. But a handful of us are spared to meet here to-day. Since this reunion was proposed, two members have passed away, one of whom, Mr. Elliot of Greenfield, was a member of the committee of arrangements.

"It is related in the history of Hawley that bears troubled the early settlers of that town, and that at a bear-hunt the brute seized a lad, and would have torn him to pieces had not one sturdy, cool-headed man, with more presence of mind than his comrades, stepped forward and planted his axe in bruin's head. A grandson of that noble old man, who had scarcely passed his majority, cast his first vote for freedom forty years ago; and since then, like his grandfather, his axe has been uplifted against every form of evil, and he has held a position in society which we all might envy, and is the pride of his neighborhood and town. His name is George D. Crittenden of Buckland, and he has been selected to preside over this meeting to-day."

Mr. Crittenden in assuming the chair addressed the company as "Ladies, gentlemen, and fellow-cranks." He then spoke of the formation of the Free Soil party and its purpose to break the slave power, which not only controlled the two great parties, but the Supreme Court as well. The effort at that time by the pro-slavery leaders was to make their institution national instead of local; and conscientious men decided to make a stand against its evil influence and power. He introduced as the first speaker Samuel D. Bardwell, Esq., of Shelburne Falls, a man who had never belonged to either of the great parties. Mr. B. said it was not unpleasant to go on exhibition as a curiosity. He was happy as he looked back across the lapse of half a century to see the wonderful progress that had been made. Massachusetts, admitted to be the banner State for liberty, was called upon fifty-two years ago to indorse an order from five or six legislatures of Southern States to enact a law to make it a penal offence to discuss the question of slavery. Governor Everett, in addressing the Legislature, said the Antislavery Society by discussing the question of slavery had made themselves amenable to the common law. The political leaders and the theological world were silenced. Mr. Bardwell said that the Antislavery movement started in the Lane Seminary, in the suburbs of Cincinnati, in 1834. Dr. Beecher was president of the school and Calvin E. Stowe a professor. The discussion among the students of the question of slavery was attended with such excitement that the seminary was broken up. Among the pupils was James G. Birney, who came from a slave State and was himself a slave-holder. He was so impressed with the discussion that he emancipated his slaves, and was obliged to leave his State, going to Ohio and then to New York. He became the standard-bearer of the Free Soilers and an earnest and powerful worker in their cause.

The president stated that there were six men in Charlemont who voted for James G. Birney, of whom one, Warren Albee, was introduced as a man almost eighty years old. Mr. A. said he could not hear what was said, but he wanted to see the brethren once more. He related some very amusing incidents of his Antislavery days. R. N. Oakman, of Montague, followed with reminiscences which went back to Jackson, and reviewed the history of the Free Soilers until they were merged into the Republican party in 1856.

A poem written by Dr. C. L. Fisk, Sr., was read by Secretary Johnson, the doctor being unable to attend the reunion. A vote of thanks was passed for the poem on motion of A. C. Parsons, of Northfield. The next speaker was George W. Mirick of Shelburne Falls, who had a very vivid recollection of the Antislavery days. His account of the attempt to excommunicate Antislavery men from the church in West Brookfield, where he then resided, was exceedingly interesting, and showed the bitter feeling that then existed against those who had the courage to declare their convictions. Dr. Josiah Trow, of Buckland, spoke well in his hearty, earnest way, and told how glad he was to meet the men with whom he labored for the right forty years ago. If there are any people on earth who have a right to be happy and rejoice it is the Free Soilers, and he was in it all over.

Rev. J. F. Moors, D.D., of Greenfield, was then introduced, and said the first lecture he ever gave was in Medfield, with the cause of Antislavery for his subject. The first petition he signed after being ordained at Deerfield was that of the three thousand ministers who asked Congress for the abolition of slavery. He voted for Martin Van Buren in 1848, with his Antislavery friends, though it came across the grain.

The Secretary announced the recent deaths of two of the original band of Free Soilers, William Elliot, of Greenfield, and U. T. Darling, Sr., of Leyden, and out of respect to them, at his suggestion, the company arose and sang "Nearer, my God, to Thee!"

Hon. A. C. Parsons, of Northfield, who has represented his district in the House of Representatives and the county in the Senate, was next introduced; and he was followed by H. S. Ranney of Ashfield, Samuel Stowell of New Salem (he was sent to the Legislature as a Free Soil member), Hopkins Woods of Greenfield, James Childs of Deerfield, Cephas Porter of Leverett, L. S. Abell of Conway (whose father was a station agent of the "underground railroad"), E. G. Wood of Shutesbury, Rev. S. Barber of Bernardston, and Jonathan Johnson of Greenfield; but want of space will not permit us to report more fully what was said. A little discussion came up as to which was the banner Free Soil town of the county. H. S. Ranney showed that Ashfield carried off the palm. In 1848 she cast 153 Free Soil votes, — more than was given to both the other parties, — and she sent a Free Soil member to the Legislature. In 1850 she cast 147 Free Soil votes, to 122 for Briggs and 43 for Boutwell, and again elected a Free Soil Representative, as she did in 1851 (when Mr. Ranney was elected), and in 1853.

The meeting throughout was of the most interesting character and greatly enjoyed. It was finally adjourned to meet annually hereafter, with the same committee of arrangements for next year, Hopkins Woods of Greenfield, and L. S. Abell of Conway being added.

THE END.

www.ingramcontent.com/pod-product-compliance
Lightning Source LLC
Chambersburg PA
CBHW021420090426
42742CB00009B/1199